NORVAL MORRISSEAU AND THE EMERGENCE OF
THE IMAGE MAKERS

NORVAL MORRISSEAU AND THE EMERGENCE OF
THE IMAGE MAKERS
ELIZABETH McLUHAN AND TOM HILL

Art Gallery of Ontario

Methuen
Toronto New York
London Sydney

The Art Gallery of Ontario gratefully acknowl-
edges the generous support of Seven-Up
Canada Inc. and Benson & Hedges (Canada)
Inc.

The Art Gallery of Ontario is funded by the Prov-
ince of Ontario, the Ministry of Citizenship and
Culture, the Municipality of Metropolitan Toronto,
and the Government of Canada through the
National Museums Corporation and the Canada
Council.

Itinerary of the Exhibition

Art Gallery of Ontario, Toronto
February 18 – April 15, 1984

Thunder Bay National Exhibition
Centre and Centre for Indian Art
May 10 – June 17, 1984

Chatham Cultural Centre
July 6 – July 29, 1984

Art Gallery of Algoma, Sault Ste. Marie
September 20 – October 21, 1984

Laurentian University Museum & Arts Centre,
Sudbury
December 19, 1984 – January 13, 1985

Copyright © 1984 Art Gallery of Ontario
ISBN: 0-458-97390-4

Canadian Cataloguing in Publication Data
McLuhan, Elizabeth.
   Norval Morrisseau and the emergence of the image
makers

Catalogue of an exhibition held at the Art Gallery of
Ontario, Feb. 18 – Apr. 15, 1984 and travelling to other
galleries.
Bibliography: p.
ISBN 0-458-97390-4

1. Indians of North America – Ontario – Art –
Exhibitions.   2. Painting, Canadian – Ontario –
Exhibitions.   3. Painting, Modern – 20th century –
Ontario – Exhibitions.   I. Hill, Tom.   II. Art Gallery
of Ontario.   III. Title.

ND246.05M44 1984   759.11'3'08997   C84-098165-1

Printed and bound in Canada
1 2 3 4 5 88 87 86 85 84

On the cover:
Saul Williams
Homage to Morrisseau 1979-80
Acrylic on canvas board
59.0 × 50.0 cm
Private Collection

Dedicated to the memory of our fathers,
Herbert Marshall McLuhan and Alton Vernon Hill

Indian Reserves of Ontario

Reserves

Reserves mentioned in text

1 Sandy Lake
2 Weagamow Lake
3 Red Lake
4 Fort William
5 Sand Point

6 Longlake 58
7 Longlake 77
8 West Bay
9 Wikwemikong
10 Six Nations

Contents

Foreword

At Seven-Up Canada Inc. and Benson & Hedges (Canada) Inc., operating companies of Philip Morris Incorporated, we expect our business activities to make social sense and our social activities to make business sense. We firmly believe that arts and business should go hand in hand, a partnership that enhances the vitality of each.

All phases of our companies' operations, from product design to packaging, from promotions to advertising, deal with the visual arts – lines, movement, design, colour, shape, sound, themes, textures, and content. Art teaches us to look at everything in a completely new manner. It converts Benson & Hedges and Seven-Up into creative mass-marketing organizations.

A sense of responsibility to the community enables Seven-Up Canada Inc. and Benson & Hedges (Canada) Inc. to manage our growth in a manner responsive to the needs of society. In short, if a company takes from the community, it must also give. And so it is that Benson & Hedges (Canada) Inc. and Seven-Up Canada Inc. have sponsored the exhibition, *Norval Morrisseau and the Emergence of the Image Makers*.

The Woodland school is recognized as a particular Canadian art form, or movement, evolving from the contemporary artist Norval Morrisseau. Over the past twenty years, six or more senior image makers have followed Morrisseau's innovations. The exhibition consists of almost fifty works from various private and public collections. It opens in February 1984 at the Art Gallery of Ontario and subsequently will be moved throughout the Ontario community, where it will be on display at such locales as Thunder Bay, Sault Ste. Marie, Sudbury, and Chatham.

Seven-Up Canada Inc. and Benson & Hedges (Canada) Inc. take pride in presenting the exhibition to these communities.

J. Wayne Mailloux,
President,
Seven-Up Canada Inc.

William H. Webb,
President,
Benson & Hedges (Canada) Inc.

Preface

Norval Morrisseau over the past quarter century has established a secure place in the history of mid-twentieth-century Canadian art. His work has been the subject of numerous exhibitions, and his supporters – as articulate as they are passionate in the cases of Selwyn Dewdney and Jack Pollock – have encouraged him in articles and book-length studies. On the other hand, there has been a wide range of opinion concerning the Canadian Native artists who have responded to his example – the so-called Woodland school – with exaggerated claims at one extreme and prejudiced dismissal at the other.

The Art Gallery of Ontario has for some time recognized the need to establish a critical framework for the evaluation of this aspect of current artistic activity in our province. Although it does not fall within the chronological period of concern of the Curator of Canadian Historical Art, personal interest led me to assume responsibility for the project. I approached Elizabeth McLuhan, a trained scholar in the field, and Tom Hill, an artist and curator with wide practical experience, asking them to evaluate the work of the artists loosely defined as "Woodland" as a phenomenon of the contemporary cultural scene. They agreed to prepare an exhibition and a book that would describe this phenomenon, its genesis and growth, considering the forces that bear upon it and the direction it is taking. They have produced a relatively small, tightly focussed exhibition that directly addresses these fundamental issues, and suggests as well the meaning this art holds for the Indian audience, and the importance it can have for the non-Indian audience for whom, by and large, it has been produced.

Although the exhibition and attendant publication are not large, the organization of this project has been complex. The dedicated commitment of Tom Hill and Elizabeth McLuhan has been the engine propelling it to successful completion, but many organizations and individuals have helped keep the course true. In particular, the boards of the Woodland Indian Cultural Educational Centre in Brantford and of the Thunder Bay National Exhibition Centre and Centre for Indian Art have supported the project generously. The co-operation of the Ojibwe Cultural Foundation of West Bay, Manitoulin Island, has also been important.

James and Carey Richards of the Legacy Gallery, Toronto, Gerald McMaster, Curator of Contemporary Indian Art at the Museum of Man in Ottawa, Jim Wright, Director of Programme Services of the Department of Indian and Northern Affairs, also in Ottawa, Patricia Ainslie, Acting Head, Art Department, at the Glenbow Museum in Calgary, Alberta, and Dr. E.S. Rogers, Curator, Department of Ethnology, Royal Ontario Museum, gave crucial help when it was needed. Collectors, all of them pioneers, have been essential to both the preliminary research and the mounting of the exhibition. The lenders should not only be congratulated for the courage of their convictions, but also thanked for their generosity in selflessly offering up treasured possessions for the edification of a varied public. The organizers would like to thank Susan Ross, Rya Levitt, Professor Doug Saunders, Dr. H.T. Schwarz, Dr. Bernhard Cinader, Miss Helen Band, John Vincett and Pamela Wheaton, Dr. Peter Lewin, Clifford and Eleanor Whetung, Bert Curtis, Professor Roz Vanderburgh, and Beth Southcott for special help.

At the Art Gallery of Ontario, the great task of co-ordination has fallen almost entirely upon Edie Sersta, Secretary to the Curator of Canadian Historical Art. She has surpassed her usual high standards. Other staff members, including the following, have also performed their tasks with professional skill and effectiveness: Barry Simpson, Manager of Curatorial Administration; Marie DunSeith, Development Manager; Maia-Mari Sutnik, Co-ordinator of Photographic Services; Larry Ostrom, Head Photographer; Elizabeth Addison, Marketing Manager, and her staff in Promotion, particularly Ivan Holmes, Design Supervisor; Eva Robinson, Registrar, and her staff; Ches Taylor, Manager of Technical Services; John Ruseckas, Chief Preparator, and his staff. It has been a pleasure working with Methuen on this publication, particularly because it has given me the opportunity to benefit again from the organizational and editorial skills of Denise Bukowski.

Every contemporary exhibition must begin and end with the artists, and in this case they have been unfailing in their general encouragement and in their personal support of the organizers. The results, we hope, repay their trust.

Dennis Reid,
Curator of Canadian Historical Art,
Art Gallery of Ontario

Indian Art in Canada: An Historical Perspective
Tom Hill

It may seem surprising that Indian art in Canada has had such a long struggle for recognition. There are a number of reasons for this neglect. First and foremost, the term "Indian art" has been carelessly defined to include those many and varied arts and crafts that have been created by Indians to reflect their traditional cultures. It is important for the understanding of Indian art that the period of time be specified when discussing any work, because since the time of European contact there has been no "pristine" Indian art that has never been modified or influenced by the dominant Euro-Canadian culture.

This essay explores three areas of Indian art — ceremonial art, the crafted arts, and the new art, examining some of the forces that eventually led to the recognition and recent acceptance of Indian art. It is intended to provide an historical perspective to the development of Indian art generally in Canada, and more specifically to provide the historical context for the acceptance of the style of painting originated by Norval Morrisseau.

1   Ceremonial Art: Form and Function

There is little recorded evidence to indicate when the North American Indian artist actually began manipulating European materials to produce fine art as "art for art's sake." There were few aboriginal art forms that were without an established function in cultural life. To the North American Indian, everything he made served a purpose. The idea of hanging a painting on a wall or mounting a sculpture on a pedestal just to admire it was completely foreign to him. That is not to say that the Indian did not enjoy having beautiful things about him. In fact, almost everything he made was decorated in some way; religious articles were often characterized by more inventive artistic interpretations than the secular objects were. Where the environment afforded more leisure time, as in the case of the northwest coast and the eastern woodland, the secular art objects became highly developed artistically and well integrated into the society.

One of the earliest accounts of an Indian painting a picture by using European materials to produce fine art, in the sense of "art for art's sake," comes from about 1840. Zacharie Vincent, a Huron Indian from the village of Lorette near Quebec, became so fascinated by his portrait being painted by Antoine Plamondon, a noted portrait painter of the time, that he promptly rendered several copies of the portrait for his own gratification. According to J. Russell Harper in *Painting in Canada*:

> Plamondon is said to have given him advice, but throughout he remained a primitive, adding detail to detail with little regard for the final artistic effect.

The Huron Indian went on to paint some highly coloured landscapes of Lorette, now in the Quebec Museum, one of which is a free copy of a Krieghoff canvas.

"Art for art's sake," as interpreted by Zacharie Vincent in his paintings, was an unusual instance of one culture observing another and adapting. For whatever reason Zacharie Vincent chose to render the paintings, his interest was short-lived and his accumulated knowledge as a painter apparently influenced no one.

Since the time of European contact, the Indians living in British North America have adapted to the predominant taste of the Western world. Usually, the adaptation of one form of artistic expression to another is relatively simple, as in the case of Zacharie Vincent or in the applied arts. But when the expression is an integral part of the total cultural environment, as with ceremonial or ritual art, the adaptation is sometimes difficult.

Near the end of the nineteenth century, such eminent scholars as Claude Lévi-Strauss and Franz Boas sought to clarify the meaning of ceremonial art within a traditional culture through their research with the Indian bands on the northwest coast of British Columbia. Their analysis of the art forms stressed the interplay of the Indian's religious world with their art. Claude Lévi-Strauss states in *The Savage Mind* that:

> A vase, a box, a wall are not independent, pre-existing objects which are subsequently decorated. They acquire their definitive existence only through the integration of the decoration with the utilitarian function. Thus, the chests of the Northwest Coast art are not merely containers embellished with a painted or carved animal. They are the animal itself, keeping an active watch over the ceremonial ornaments which have been entrusted to its care. Structure modifies decoration, but decoration is the final cause of structure, which must also adapt itself to the requirements of the former. The final product is a whole: utensil-ornament, object-animal, box that speaks.

The Indian artist strove to integrate the relevant traditional elements of his culture into the material at hand, in an attempt to create a form that gave concrete expression to these elements. The artist, in seeking to create a functioning whole structure, was also aware, as is any artist, of the subtleties of form and style. The successful creation combined both the cultural association common to all community members with the successful rendering of the material with which the artist worked.

One need only examine the Iroquois false face mask (fig. 1) to view the integration of form and function in art. The false face mask is carved directly from the trunk of a living softwood tree and depicts a supernatural being common to the whole community. Once the image is completed in relief on the side of the tree, it is carefully removed and finished with pigments and animal hair. Medicine bags may be added and attached to the false face to increase its powers. The face is created for a healing ceremony, and the person who wears the mask does so to focus the attention of the viewers on the power of the supernatural forces, rather than the mask image itself. The wearer, through dance and sounds, imitates the supernatural being that it depicts, thus integrating the false face into a functioning drama or healing ritual. Claude Lévi-Strauss was to define this principle as "metonymy," wherein a part symbolizes the whole.

The understanding of Iroquoian mythology does not readily lead to the total appreciation of Iroquoian aesthetic expression. The importance inherent in the artist's representation of his mythological consciousness lies primarily in the

fig. 1 Contemporary false face mask from the Collection of the Woodland Indian Cultural Educational Centre, Brantford.

sacred essence of the myth, rather than the literal rendering of it. Through the realization of the false face, the artist and the viewer are able to transcend both time and space as the artist brings his mythological past into the realistic present in the form of a false face, which acts as both utensil and supernatural being.

The ceremonial arts such as the false faces from southern Ontario, the masks and regalia from the northwest coast of British Columbia, the medicine bundle charms from the Prairies, and the birch bark Midewiwin Society scrolls from northwestern Ontario served a necessary function in religious ceremonies within Indian communities. All drew their power from the shared belief in the image, and from the quality and interpretive skill of the artist. These ceremonial arts, which manifested the traditional religion and culture, were the least compatible with European concepts. Consequently, they were to receive the most destructive blows from the impact of the European colonizers.

By the nineteenth century in British North America, the Christian missionaries were firmly established, each sect having staked out its specific territory, complete with its own particular set of Indians. As a result, by Confederation the ceremonial arts were in rapid decline. What remained of the Indian cultural tradition after the missionaries' thorough scouring of paganism was then subjected to the Canadian government's continuing and official policy of assimilation. This assimilationist policy was manifested through enactment of the Indian Act of 1874, the federal legislation designed to regulate every element of Indian life on "reserves," including those remnants of land that remained under Indian control. On April 19, 1884, assent was given to amend the act to prohibit the potlatch. The original statement in Section III reads as follows:

> Every Indian or other person who engages in or assists in celebrating the Indian festival known as the Potlach [sic] or in the Indian dance known as the Tamanawas is guilty of a misdemeanour, and shall be liable to an imprisonment for a term of not more than 6 nor less than 2 months in any gaol or other place of confinement; and any Indian or other person who encourages, either directly or indirectly, an Indian or Indians to get up such a festival or dance or to celebrate the same or who shall assist in the celebration of same is guilty of a like offense, and shall be liable to the same punishment.

In the statutes of Canada of 1926-27, a new provision to the act outlawed the sundance, a ritual practised by those bands living on the Prairies. While there were no specific references to the Midewiwin and longhouse rituals in Ontario, the law did, however, give the missionaries and the civil servants a mandate to pursue an aggressive acculturation program. No other revisions were made to this section until it was completely removed from the Indian Act in 1951.

The Potlatch Law, as it came to be called, had a profound effect on the artistic expression of Indian artists. In most cases the artists' creations were an integral part of such forbidden ceremonies. Not only was the artist the producer of the objects used in these now-forbidden rites, but often he was also the philosopher who initiated the change that kept the ceremonial traditions viable and evolving. The condemnation of the Indians' traditional spiritual life forced the artist either to find other ways to express his creativeness or to conform to the prescribed artistic forms established by the Euro-Canadians. Consequently, the long and sacred traditions that were the roots of ceremonial art ebbed to an unforgivable low as the artists passively accepted the Euro-Canadians' aesthetic tastes, their culture, and their established order.

2 The Crafted Arts: Towards Commercialization

"Acculturation" is a term often used to suggest debasement when referring to the style of art produced by North American Indians. For the applied arts or crafts, acculturation began from the time of the first European contact, with the introduction of new materials and technology. As Nelson Graburn has shown, two societies that are in contact with each other over a long period of time and are at greatly different technological and economic levels will eventually exchange materials, items, and ideas. Very little is known of the acculturation process that occurred among the various Indian nations in prehistoric times. Archaeologists, of course, have given some indication, gained from material culture recovered from various prehistoric sites, that trade did occur. Unfortunately, the only materials retrieved from these sites are usually non-perishable items such as shells, bones, stones, or ceramics. We can only speculate that if trade was taking place, techniques and artistic styles in Indian arts would have also been modified.

The technology and the new materials introduced by the colonizers were readily accepted by the Indians as more functional. The colonial powers gave these new materials as tokens to win the friendship and alliance of the Indian nations, and in some instances to buy their lands. To the European encountering Indian arts, they presented a colourful and exotic display that impressed but did not involve him. There is no doubt that the aesthetic concepts involved in this work were too foreign and far-removed from his own; also, the European did not consider the Indian to be his intellectual equal. After they overcame their initial revulsion towards the culture, Europeans collected arts and crafts as souvenirs. A survey of North American artifacts in Europe can attest to these early souvenir collectors, from the Russian sea captains sailing between Russian America and their homeland in the early eighteenth century to the British military in the service of the empire. Norman Feder notes in *Two Hundred Years of North American Indian Art*:

> Almost from the time of first European contact, it was the habit of travellers visiting Indian groups to collect souvenirs as mementoes of their trips. The Indians were quick to realise the commercial potentialities of this tourist trade and very soon started making articles specifically for this purpose. Initially there was little difference in the quality of materials of these pieces, since they were following old traditions. Most Indians, however, soon realised that the travellers were willing to accept inferior materials, and they often preferred novelties which could be simply and inexpensively produced.

This realization of the commercial aspect of arts and crafts was never more evident that in the development of argillite carving by the Haidas of the Queen Charlotte Islands. Conceived and developed during the mid-nineteenth century totally for the white market, the carvings are made from slate-like stone that can be carved and polished to a highly glossy finish. They had no function in traditional Haida society, primarily since once the stone hardens, it is brittle and shatters easily; it could not be used in any capacity that required strength and durability. The flourishing of the art form depended totally on its success in the marketplace, which was created completely outside Haida society. Ironically, while argillite carving was gaining success, the Canadian government was outlawing by statute the very essence of Haida society, the potlatch.

The popularity of argillite carving in Victorian Canada is a good indication of the general attitude of Canadians towards the country's diminishing Indian populations. They viewed the carvings simply as curios, remnants of a dying

people. Little interest was shown in the culture and mythology that was often vividly expressed. Carol Sheehan has noted in *Pipes That Won't Smoke, Coal That Won't Burn*:

> The subject matter of the carvings and the meanings they represented were apparently not part of the purchase price; indeed they probably were not even taken into consideration. The fact that the subject matter went through several drastic changes with little or no change in its acceptance by the market would seem to indicate this. Furthermore, the scarceness of museum documentation for argillite sculpures might be another indication that the buyer was more interested in the fact that it was carved by an Indian than in the meaning of its images.

Little attention was given to these argillite images by the consumer; ironically, this art form reflected the paganism that the Victorian consumers, along with their missionaries, adamantly opposed and worked ceaselessly to eradicate. A reflection of the prevalent attitude appeared in 1900 in an article written by Marshall Scott in *The Canadian Magazine*. In his piece of sensational journalism, the writer described "the ghoulish pagan practices," and implied that there was both a sense of duty and repulsion among whites concerning primitive people. As Ronald Haycock records in *The Image of the Indian* (1971), Marshall indicated that pagans made up 30 per cent of Canadian aboriginals, but civilization was winning its way, and old pagans of inferior blood were dying out faster than men of good race who wished to improve themselves.

The late nineteenth and early twentieth centuries saw the proliferation of other Indian curios developed solely for the souvenir market (fig. 2). Sometimes called "whimsies," the beaded velvet pin cushions shaped like high-button shoes, hearts, flowers, ladies' hats, and parasols, the elaborate beaded picture frames and the multi-shaped forms that did not identify one thing or another but simply announced the place and date of purchase can still be found throughout antique stores in Canada. These souvenirs reflected the elaborate and ornate style preferred by Victorians; they had no style or tradition that identified them as Indian except for the technique of beading, which in the minds of many Canadians was now synonymous with Indians. Like argillite carvings, these newly crafted forms depended on the development of new audiences at about the time their own craft products were becoming obsolete in Indian communities across Canada. Functions and forms were redefined and economic production motives replaced the utilitarian ones of the past. New marketing systems evolved from the demands of travelling medicine shows, which employed Indian people; from the railroad tourist trade, which brought the tourist in direct contact with the romanticized version of an Indian; and from the popular interest of Canadians in exhibitions and agricultural fairs, which provided the main outlet for the selling of these objects. The interest of the white consumer played a major role in the creative moulding of these souvenir products, merely by the acceptance of them. To the Indian, the admiration of the white consumer was an important factor because it gave approval to their "Indianness," which in all other areas was condemned.

The condemnation of the Indians' cultural traditions was centred in the Indian Affairs Department in Ottawa, with its well-intentioned goal of raising the Indian to levels of civilization fashioned on the Christian ethic. Having common objectives with the Anglican, Methodist, and Roman Catholic churches, the Indian Affairs department established education programs that would eventually "civilize" their "wards." These programs were planned with the objective of breaking up Indian societal relationships by removing their traditional patterns, values, and habits, and replacing them with those of the European. One method was the establishment of residential schools far away from Indian communities, in order to isolate at an early age the children from their parents, with their traditional habits and customs. The speaking of any Native language was forbidden; visits home were discouraged.

Support and encouragement for this acculturation policy was never more clearly delineated than in Marshall Scott's 1900 article in *The Canadian Magazine*, which stated:

> The Queen's representatives in Canada have known how to keep faith with and earn the confidence of the red man, and the servants of the Most High have shrunk from no sacrifice to perform their imposed duty of winning the pagans.

Understandably, then, the interest in developing the Indian arts-and-crafts market received no attention from Indian Affairs. It wasn't until a group of concerned Montreal women formed the Women's Art Association of Montreal in 1900, which six years later became the Canadian Handicraft Guild, that ardent support for the commercialization of Indian arts and crafts took shape. After organizing exhibitions (fig. 3), travelling shows, and competitions for Indian people the guild eventually, through their "Indian Committee," became a lobbying organization on behalf of Indian craftsmen for craft programs established by the government.

The ultimate objective of this philanthropic organization was "to encourage, retain, revise, and develop Canadian Handicrafts and Art Industries throughout the Dominion," according to Virginia Watt in her essay in *Canadian Guild of Crafts, Quebec*. Among the first members of the Canadian Handicraft Guild were people who had collections of Indian and Eskimo crafts; so it was not surprising that one of the guild's interests was to encourage the Native people of Canada to create good traditional crafts. To the guild the preservation of Indian culture was of prime importance. The arts and crafts were, in their viewpoint, inseparable from the culture; if the arts and crafts were permitted to die, so part of the culture would die also. Little did they realize that their efforts to create a

fig. 3 Indian art exhibition sponsored by the Women's Art Association of Montreal, 1905.

viable commercial market would also encourage the evolution of a style far removed from any traditional trait of Indian societies.

The Canadian Handicraft Guild was not the only organization involved in the promotion of Indian arts and crafts through exhibitions and competitions. A similar organization, the Society for the Furtherance of B.C. Indian Arts and Crafts, spearheaded by Alice Ravenhill, was founded in Victoria in 1940. Miss Ravenhill states in *Memoirs of an Educational Pioneer* that:

> The organization objects were summarized as constructive, cultural, and economic; these being based upon adequate evidence of the inherited artistic gifts and mechanical and manual dexterities latent in young Indians, shown in painting, carving, modelling, in drama, dancing, singing, and also in mechanical abilities of a high order.

Miss Ravenhill's efforts to promote Indian arts on the west coast did not receive the same positive responses that the Canadian Handicraft Guild had in the east. Miss Ravenhill remarked that the "attendance was the smallest on record" at speeches she made on west-coast art at the Victoria Arts and Crafts Society, the Women's University Club in Victoria, and the Businessmen's Lunch Club. However, all her efforts did not go unnoticed. In September 1945 an article in *Saturday Night* paid tribute to her work. The writer claimed that the exhibition of modern Indian arts and crafts, organized with the help of Ravenhill at the Provincial Museum in Victoria, "had preserved much that was beautiful in Indian Culture and, indeed had encouraged a revival in art that might have succumbed had it not been for her efforts."

In 1935 the Canadian Handicraft Guild, in promoting Indian arts and crafts, circulated a questionnaire to Indian agents across Canada to determine the state of the arts-and-crafts industry. According to Eleanor Verbicky in *The Creative Tradition* (1982), results of the survey, reported in 1936, "indicated the rapid decline of good work with the advance of 'civilization,' but agreed that with discerning encouragement much could still be saved, especially if increased markets could be found." As a result of the survey and the lobbying efforts of the guild, the Indian Affairs department in Ottawa established the Medical Welfare and Training Division in 1936, with the mandate to provide programs for the encouragement of arts and crafts and the sale of handicrafts, along with its other responsibilities for schools, employment, health care, and agricultural projects. Very few changes were made in program objectives over the years, until 1969, when the department went through a major reorganization. Personnel were reassigned from the Northern Affairs Program to Indian Affairs, creating the Indian Eskimo Economic Development Branch.

During the forties and fifties, these philanthropic organizations directly or indirectly influenced the artistic development of Indian and Eskimo communities across Canada. The evolution of the crafted arts towards commercialization in Canada was a direct outcome of the programs initiated by these organizations. On the west coast, the Society for the Furtherance of B.C. Indian Arts and Crafts paternalistically continued its Indian art exhibition program. In the Victoria *Colonist*, Dr. Clifford Carl, representative of the society and the Director of the Provincial Museum, stated in 1944:

> We must first encourage these arts and crafts in the Indians and then bring them to the attention of the public. One of the chief characteristics of the Indian is his urge to create and ornament. The old ceremonies have gone too but the ability is still there, and only needs stimulus.

Both the Canadian Handicraft Guild and the Society for the Furtherance of B.C. Indian Arts and Crafts had a direct line through their membership to the political establishment in Ottawa, and as a result were able to effect a number of major policy changes. The guild, because of its geographic proximity to Ottawa, was more successful as a lobbying organization for federal programs. One must remember that in the fifties, status Indians still did not have the right to vote federally, and many Indian communities were just beginning to become conscious of their ability to influence the Canadian political system through lobbying.

Where Indian communities had direct access to southern markets and a surviving traditional culture, some artistic development took place. For example, at Ohsweken near Brantford the Six Nations Arts Council was formed in 1957. This community organization sponsored oil painting classes, an annual spring exhibition, and an arts-and-crafts sale, and served as a lobbying organization for an art gallery and cultural centre. Its realm of influence was really centred in its own community, although in the early sixties the council did acquire a few works from Indian artists outside the Six Nations for its permanent collection. It had little impact on national cultural programs, however. In fact, the organization was labelled "too nationalistic" by the local Indian agent, who had the authority at Six Nations to redirect a cultural grant designated to the council to another organization on the reserve involved in sports – which he did.

The Canadian Handicraft Guild's greatest contribution in the commercialization of the crafted arts was its role in the development of the Eskimo Arts Program. In March 1939 the Indian Committee of the guild was changed to the Indian and Eskimo Committee so that the scope of the guild could be extended to encourage Eskimo crafts. As Virginia Watt reports in *Canadian Guild of Crafts, Quebec*, in the same year David McKeand, of the Northwest Territories Administration Office, who also was a committee member, reported to the guild that "poor hunting years in the North caused acute suffering and deprivation among the people and that this condition might be alleviated by developing a market for Eskimo crafts in the south."

Perhaps hindered by the outbreak of World War II, only a small number of

fig. 4 Inuit soapstone sculpture of Elvis Presley, c. 1963.

craft-collection programs in the north were initiated. It wasn't until the arrival of James Houston, an artist and teacher from Grandmère, Quebec, in 1948 that the developmental program actually got off the ground. Sponsored by the guild, James Houston travelled to Port Harrison and Povungnituk in an effort to promote the production of crafts. It was the enthusiastic efforts of Miss Alice Lighthall, Chairman of the Indian and Eskimo Committee, that finally encouraged the government to take on the responsibility of an Eskimo arts program. By the end of the fifties, the Eskimo arts co-operative movement was well established, with a dynamic national and international promotion program geared to convincing buyers that these works produced in the north were in fact not souvenirs of a dying culture, but art.

The promotion campaign developed by the Northern Program was extensive and was carefully synchronized with the market's expansion. Aleksandrs Sprudzs, the co-operative development officer for the Northern Program, described in a 1975 report the scope of the promotion, which consisted of:

> Exhibitions and Art Shows in Canada and across the globe, sponsored publicity trips by artists and craft producers, establishment and protection of trademarks, symbols, and copyrights, exposure of the Arctic products at official government functions, setting up of advisory bodies and ad-hoc committees, even for a while being a distributor of arts and crafts, the final result of which was a creation and support of a special marketing organization.

If items did not reflect the required "primitiveness" that was being promoted in the marketplace, they were destroyed. According to Sprudzs, in the initial stages of the co-operative movement a government-employed arts-and-crafts specialist edited the objects out if they did not meet the workmanship, quality, and market standards. One such item that did not meet the market standards was a soapstone sculpture of Elvis Presley (fig. 4); it was rescued from the sledgehammer by a public servant who felt the piece reflected the reality of the Sugluk community with which he was so familiar. Since these production centres were conceived as co-operatives, with the passing of time, Sprudzs reported, "more and more of such responsibilities were handed over to the local people who had shown interest and leadership qualities."

Jacqueline Fry described in an *artscanada* article the fact that Eskimo art is usually analyzed in European terms as "primitive art," and as a result it is generally treated as "an annex to the European cultural tradition." She continues:

> Occidentals seem to seek in the primitive arts a set of qualities that correspond to their idea of traditional primitive life. The objects are considered valid or authentic only if they have served in religious, magic, or even political functions, but the very notions of these functions lack roots in reality. Any object that does not fit the standard notions is rejected as inauthentic.

Using her analysis of the general attitude or the preconceptions that the Euro-Canadian had of the emerging art forms, it is easy to understand in economic terms the government's decision to maintain such unusual art-market standards, which negated individualism and encouraged a collective ethnicity.

The passage of time has seen the Eskimo art co-operatives recognizing and publicizing individual artists. For those concerned with the aesthetics of the art form, this recognition has been undoubtedly beneficial; for those concerned with the dynamics of an economic co-operative it could only have been detrimental, since such emphasis on the individual would have been bound to create tensions within a precariously evolving group.

3 The New Art: Politics and Pictographs

In 1960 Canada gave Indian people the right to vote, and began to regard them as equal within the Canadian political system. It was the beginning of the socially conscious sixties, and Indian communities across the nation began speaking out against their tragic social conditions. Improved communications made the Indians aware of the political activities of other minorities, such as the Quiet Revolution in Quebec and the civil rights movement in the United States. Harold Cardinal wrote of these groups in *The Unjust Society*:

> We have measured their success and their failure. . . . These things too are our classrooms now and our textbooks. And we are learning our lessons well.

While the Indian communities raced towards gaining more political control over the economic, educational, and social aspects of their lives, the Indian artists, perhaps because they did not want to alienate buyers, appeared to be satisfied with minority status as Indians and as artists. They saw no reason to take any political action to find a role for themselves in the new order, and consequently much of their art did not reflect social or political comment. The new art fostered individualism but favoured a highly identifiable Indian content. From a national perspective, Indian artists expressed themselves in a variety of styles, from northwest-coast graphics and traditional sculpture to the pictorial themes of artists of the Prairies and the image makers of northwestern Ontario. The image-making movement was given birth by the imaginative genius of Norval Morrisseau, with his first exhibition at the Pollock Gallery in 1962. These startling, vivid new images enshrined the traditional Cree-Ojibwa* culture and became a pioneering force for a whole host of Cree-Ojibwa painters who imitated Morrisseau's style. By the end of the sixties "the Morrisseau school" was firmly established, and epitomized Indian nationalism well into the seventies.

Although willing to accept Indian art as an expression of its identity, the Indian community during the sixties did not provide the market, primarily because neither individuals nor institutions in the community enjoyed an economic base sufficient to enable them to become collectors of their own people's art. At the same time, once an Indian artist began to achieve some degree of economic success, he was often accused of selling his culture to the white man. The Indian artist found this kind of paradox bewildering and somewhat agonizing, since they had no control over it. In Canada, the Indian art market was ideal. Canada as a nation during the sixties was going through its own identity crisis, and the art-buying public was eager to purchase anything that reflected a Canadian consciousness. As Margaret Atwood aptly asks in her book *Survival*: "The problem is what do you do for a past if you are white, relatively new to a continent, and rootless?" In the true Canadian literary tradition, you identify with the victim; you become concerned with Canada's own survival against the cultural domination of the United States.

The need for a Canadian identity most likely influenced the art-buying public to recognize the value of traditional imagery. Certainly on the national scene "Eskimo art," now changed to "Inuit art," had already conditioned the public by establishing its market popularity for the past ten years. The Indian-art market may have also been encouraged by several events and exhibitions, such as the 1967 *Arts of the Raven* exhibition in Vancouver, the 1969 *Masterpieces of Indian and Eskimo Art* exhibition in Ottawa, and the Indians of Canada Pavilion at Expo '67 in Montreal. These geographically separated exhibitions of material culture and contemporary art further enhanced and popularized the ethnic identity for the consumer. Whether out of genuine appreciation, guilt

*Note: The spelling "Ojibwa" has been used throughout, except in the case of proper names that use the spellings "Ojibway" or "Ojibwe."

over past sins, or a need to acquire something Canadian, the art-buying public chose to look at the new art emerging from Indian communities as a significant statement from a fellow Canadian. For Norval Morrisseau, with prehistoric roots in the country and an inherent Cree-Ojibwa cosmology, his acceptance was a matter of course.

"The monolithic structure of Western industrial society . . . is itself cracking and in the ferment of change hope is springing up so that Indians too can find a place for themselves in the new order," wrote Marlene Castellano in 1972 in *The Only Good Indian*. In the sixties "the ferment of change" was never more evident in the Indian Affairs department, as the government made an effort to respond to cries of social injustice from the Indian people. On March 17, 1964, a submission was made to the Cabinet for the creation within the Department of Indian Affairs of a new division to be called "Social Programs." The submission proposed that the new Social Programs Division be responsible for developing policies and plans for welfare services, community services, and cultural affairs. The Cultural Affairs section was defined in the following manner in the Cabinet submission:

> The cultural dimension in a community development program has to be recognized, along with the social and economic dimensions. It would be desirable, therefore, to create a cultural affairs section in the division which would employ selected persons of Indian origin. The task of this staff would be to promote and facilitate the development of various forms of Indian cultural expression in the arts including painting, sculpture, music, sports, special radio and TV series and special publications. This section would also arrange scholarships in the arts, would assist in the organization of local exhibitions and other displays and provide consultation services as required on these matters. An important function of this section would be to provide leadership and encouragement to organizations active in the field of Indian arts and to maintain liaison with other voluntary agencies interested in this work.

The submission received Cabinet approval in 1964, and Walter Rudnicki was appointed the first chief of the division, with an obligation to implement the cultural program as quickly as possible. By 1966 Mr. Rudnicki departed, leaving a few public servants sincerely trying to give the Cultural Affairs section the form that had originally been intended. Unfortunately, the lack of support of senior management and the hiring of non-Indian bureaucrats unfamiliar with the traditional culture of the Indian people weakened the organization considerably. It wasn't until the Minister of Indian Affairs, Arthur Laing, decided that an Indians of Canada Pavilion should be created at Expo '67, and that the Cultural Affairs section should co-ordinate these efforts, that the division had a sense of purpose.

Expo '67 in Montreal provided the first opportunity to bring together Indian artists, Indian politicians, and federal bureaucrats in a common forum. These initial planning meetings were organized by Yves Theriault, then head of the Cultural Affairs section. It was at one of these early meetings that George Manuel, then an Indian political leader from British Columbia, attacked the department for manoeuvring Indian artists into approving the design and the theme of the pavilion. Manuel dominated these early meetings to such an extent that future planning meetings were elevated to the status of "symposia" on Indian art – thereby restricting the participation of any Indian politicians.

The majority of the Indian politicians had little or no interest in the participation of artists at Expo. In fact, some of the artists' work was considered to be *avant-garde* by the Indian communities. Indeed, to expect the politicians to give it consideration above the other pressing social and political problems of the day would have been inconsistent with the *raison d'être* of the Indian organizations.

The series of Expo consultation meetings, which were restricted to appointed Indian artists only, were also surrounded by controversy. The appropriateness of including the poetry of a non-status Indian, the appointment of a non-Indian sculptor to assist some artists with exterior murals, and the selection of more dramatic visuals that would further expose the tragic social conditions of Indian communities were some of the issues argued.

Morrisseau was selected as one of ten artists to complete one of the exterior murals on the pavilion. Unwilling to get involved in any of the political issues, he did, however – along with George Clutesi, a B.C. artist – take issue with the Cultural Affairs section, which they felt was telling them what to paint. Morrisseau and his apprentice, Carl Ray, completed one of the large murals, a sensuous earth mother with her children (fig. 5). When Expo was over, the controversial Indians of Canada Pavilion fell into disrepair and the mural passed into oblivion.

After Expo '67, the development of Indian art was overseen by the Cultural Affairs section, which became a separate division of the Department of Indian Affairs. Due to pressure from Indian politicians for an Indian person to be appointed Division Head, Yves Theriault resigned and Dr. Ahab Spence, a Cree, took over. Under Spence's direction, a study collection of Indian art was established. This included major works from Norval Morrisseau, Gerald Tailfeathers, Alex Janvier, Arthur Shilling, and Daphne Odjig. He also initiated the publication of *Tawow*, a magazine whose objective was to produce serious criticism on Indian art. The mood of the department's program for the development of Indian art may best be summed up in the words of Arthur Laing, the Minister of Indian Affairs in 1968, who said in a speech to the Vancouver Institute that year:

> We must seek out and encourage the artistic talents of young Indian people and help them express the aims and aspirations of today, not of yesterday or antiquity. We need to find more Clutesi's, more Morrisseau's, more painters, writers, and sculptors – more men like Arthur Shilling.

What the Department of Indian Affairs did not envision was that the Cultural Affairs Division would eventually take on a role comparable to a mini-Canada Council for status Indians. As limited as its expertise and financial resources were, the division was able to effect some changes in the development of Indian art. Besides publishing articles, producing exhibitions, and establishing a permanent collection, one such development program undertook a series of market evaluations on the work of Indian artists. Harry Malcolmson, one of the contractors who completed the task, states in the conclusion of *Report by Harry Malcolmson Re: Oil Paintings by Alex Janvier:*

> May I commend your vision in attempting to assist this artist and thereby enrich the art resources of this country. It seems to me you are proceeding in an intelligent and a constructive manner. I am sure your program will succeed.

Cultural Affairs' major drawback was that it was a program centred in the Department of Indian Affairs, which made it susceptible to the constantly changing political environment. For Indian artists, it encouraged the isolation of their work to such a degree that other cultural institutions that had a mandate

fig. 5 The Morrisseau mural on the Indians of Canada Pavilion at Expo '67.

for developing and encouraging Canadian art did not include Indian artists in their programs. This isolation had the effect of inhibiting the integration of Indian art into the Canadian artistic mainstream. Native art was viewed by the Canadian public as an adjunct to the arts-and-crafts marketing program, which was being revitalized down the hall in the Economic Development Branch.

As mentioned earlier, in 1969, while Cultural Affairs was struggling with its program initiatives, a major reorganization in the department reassigned personnel from the Northern Affairs program to Indian Affairs, thus creating the Indian Eskimo Economic Development Branch. The new arrivals brought with them their expertise in the marketing of Inuit art, and this expertise was a major factor in the revitalization of the Indian arts-and-crafts marketing program. In order to provide a rationale and a process for the implementation of new production and marketing programs over a five-year period, a Montreal consulting firm, Sorres Incorporated, was hired. The Sorres Report was responsible for the creation of two advisory boards, one composed of provincial Indian craftspeople and another composed of both Indian and non-Indian entrepreneurs; for the establishment of a central wholesale marketing warehouse; and for the creation of sub-programs in product development and promotion. It was the promotion sub-program that was to try to penetrate the art market on behalf of Indian artists and craftsmen. The program was based entirely on the Inuit art-marketing experience, which had proven so successful during the fifties. Its objective was to promote the distinctiveness of Indian arts and crafts, a "one-of-a-kind" sales pitch, in order to give the products the snob appeal or status requisite in the art market. Television commercials, film documentaries, exhibitions, and publications made up the program.

Not everyone was convinced that the department should be moving in this direction. The Laurentian Institute, a consulting firm for social and economic development, wrote a critical analysis of the Sorres Report. John Dockstader, an employee of the Institute, wrote in *The Indian Arts and Crafts Business*:

> The Sorres report imposes a fine mechanical structure on the arts and crafts program – but all too often, the Indian craftsman has been offered or given just such a plan for the production and marketing of his wares, and all too often he has been left with a handful of hollow hopes and bankrupt promises. He has known financial failure and he has seen his reputation as a craftsman suffer. The Indian advisory committee looks good on paper – but it will be made up primarily of retailers interested in the souvenir market and the possibilities for quick turnovers and quick profits. I am convinced it will not begin to take into account the possibilities for arts and crafts development which I think exist. I would also point out that the Sorres group is composed neither of artists, nor craftsmen, nor designers, nor do they understand the Indian mind or the Indian past.

Robert Fulford, writing in the *Toronto Star* on June 2, 1973, also detected the propagandist element in the promotion program, with its release of a book designed to popularize Indian art. Fulford stated:

> It is right and just that the federal Department of Indian Affairs and Northern Development should do what it can to explore and publicize the art of Canadian Indians. But of course a wary taxpayer who examines a lush art book like *Indian Arts in Canada* – a book heavily subsidized, so that it sells at a price much lower than any private publisher could manage, even with a Canada Council grant – can be forgiven if he sniffs the air for the scent of propaganda. After all, propaganda is one of the main functions of modern government, and it is only natural that we approach a book from Ottawa by asking: What are they trying to prove?

The book was intended to convince the public that contemporary Indian art, or the new art, existed. The consumer image was a distorted one that viewed crafts and art in the same category, an attitude encouraged by the federal marketing program. Very little effort was made to promote the art as the work of a particular individual, a necessary requirement in the understanding of the new art.

From 1970 to 1975 the marketing wholesale operation continued to grow. Handmade products arrived daily in the warehouses from Indian communities across Canada. There employees categorized them as art or craft. A whole new labelling program was introduced, utilizing the stretched beaver pelt logo, which was introduced by the department in the sixties. It was believed that the designation of a superior crafted item as art would invariably increase the monetary value of the item and bring a better return to the warehouse and the craftsmen.

Dissatisfied with the marketing directions of the government-run program, a group of Indian artists came together in Winnipeg in the early seventies under the title "The Group of Seven." Recognizing the problem their title might present, no effort was made to change it; they felt it made a political statement in itself. The period was one of considerable camaraderie among the artists, perhaps because of their isolation from the Ottawa-Toronto Indian-art scene, or perhaps because of their common battle against the department's programs. Since most of the meetings were held either in Daphne Odjig's house or print shop, she was made the unofficial head; other members included Jackson Beardy, Carl Ray, Joseph Sanchez, Eddy Cobiness, Roy Thomas, and Alex Janvier. At a later date Norval Morrisseau exhibited with the group. Besides providing a forum for criticism, the group pursued the following objectives: to organize exhibitions, to develop proposals for the establishment of an art scholarship program, and to develop a strategy that would educate the public about the individual merits of their work. The latter objective was mounted in order to oppose the marketing and promotion program, which they felt inhibited their development with its emphasis on the "Indianness" of Indian art. By 1975, the group had disbanded and the members went their separate ways; the administration of their organization had impinged on their time as artists.

One of the most important developments the federal marketing program encouraged was the public's interest in art prints. Their popularity resulted in the proliferation of silkscreen shops devoted to the reproduction of Indian works. Carolyn Hawley, in an unpublished essay on "The Marketing of Contemporary Indian Art," states:

> The painting of West Coast and Woodland art lends itself to serigraph printing since the images are characterized by a linearity and flat colour areas. A restricted palette of a few brilliant colours lowers printing costs and results in the marketing of limited-edition signed prints at affordable prices. . . . Commercially silkscreened prints have a potential for success similar to that of Inuit graphics.

One of the first silkscreen operations was organized by Daphne Odjig, the Odawa painter who began producing her own and fellow artists' work through her own shop, Odjig Indian Prints of Canada. Carl Ray and Roy Thomas joined her organization and produced a series of unnumbered prints, which were primarily directed to the souvenir market. As Odjig's product evolved from a mass-produced item to a more sophisticated signed and numbered print to suit changing market demands, she approached Bill Lobchuk of The Screen Shop in

Winnipeg to produce her work. Great Grassland Graphics, also a Winnipeg-based company, started marketing Woodland Indian silkscreen prints in limited editions.

In Ontario, with start-up grants from the Ontario and federal governments, Josh, Goyce, and Henry Kakegamic started a silkscreen shop, Triple K Co-operative, primarily to produce their own work. Located in Red Lake, Ontario, a hundred air miles north of Kenora, they began producing their own unlimited editions on cloth and paper, as well as works by Saul Williams, Paddy and Barry Peters, and Norval Morrisseau. Similar to Odjig's experience, they were soon producing limited-edition prints to meet a growing sophisticated market. Art Loft in Peterborough, Woodland Studios in Cutler, and People's Art in Ottawa, which had a wholesaling relationship with Canadian Native Prints of Vancouver, also produced silkscreen and lithographic prints.

In the mid-seventies the federal government established a wholesale operation, Canadian Indian Marketing Service, which created a fine art division to publish and market limited-edition prints for the burgeoning market. There is no doubt that this rapid growth in print shops was the direct result of Indian artists trying to respond to the market demand created by the promotional program of Indian Affairs.

In July 1975 the Arts and Crafts section, with its Central Marketing Service in the Indian Eskimo Economic Development Branch, had become the Canadian Indian Marketing Service. The same year the National Indian Advisory Committee became the National Indian Arts and Crafts Corporation (NIACC), with the objective of taking control and ownership of the Marketing Service and its programs. Carolyn Hawley summarized this period in her 1982 paper:

> The Canadian Indian Marketing Service seems to have taken up where the Central Marketing Service left off. Handled by Imanco, a management firm named by contract, the Canadian Indian Marketing Service inherited the same types of financial problems as its predecessor. The Central Marketing Service had, over a ten-year period, accumulated about $400,000 worth of inventory which had depreciated in value. The Finance and Administration Agency of the federal government would not allow the Central Indian Marketing Service to mark down these goods. Thus the company was stuck with a lot of stock, half of which was not in good condition. In 1978, the Canadian Indian Marketing Service (CIMS) was dissolved and its inventory sold by the federal government to Crown Assets Disposal Corporation.

The National Indian Arts and Crafts Corporation continued; however, its objectives changed with the government's termination of the wholesale marketing operation. NIACC is now a non-profit Indian-run organization that acts as a holding company, allocating funds from the department to provincial arts and crafts organizations. The corporation inherited the remains of the department's promotion program and now sponsors trade shows, acts as wholesaler and retailer, and sponsors Native artists and craftspeople. One of NIACC's efforts to develop a closer working relationship with Indian artists was its attempt to establish a National Indian Arts Council similar to the Canadian Eskimo Arts Council. Existing on paper only, the National Indian Arts Council never material-ized, primarily because of the difference between economic and cultural objectives.

During the same period that the federal government was establishing its programs, the Ontario provincial government was mounting similar programs to provide financial and consultative services to Indians who entered the arts-and-crafts industry. The province decided to create its own wholesale and retail marketing program. The wholesale program, Indian Crafts of Ontario, was in direct competition with the already established federal marketing service. The results were disastrous when federal and provincial wholesale buyers raced for the same product, increasing the demand and the price. Realizing their mistake, Indian Crafts of Ontario sold its stock to Ottawa and closed its doors.

In 1969 the White Paper officially titled "Statement of the Government of Canada on Indian Policy" was released, in an effort to initiate changes to promote "full and equal [Indian] participation in the cultural, social, economic, and political life of Canada." The Indian political leaders found themselves actively engaged in opposing the implementation of this new policy, fearing the possible loss of lands, rights, and their special relationship with the British Crown through the Canadian government.

The first proposal in response to the White Paper came from the Indian Association of Alberta. It was known as the Red Paper and, among other issues, it stressed the importance and uniqueness of the culture of Indian nations. As a result, the early efforts of the association in the area of Indian cultural education later blossomed into a national program of cultural educational centres, in an attempt to safeguard and enhance the development of all forms of Indian cultural expression.

In 1971 a federal cultural educational centres program was implemented, and was placed under a special secretariat and co-managed by the Department of the Secretary of State and the Department of Indian Affairs. By April 1973 the secretariat appeared to be having trouble with the program, as the gap between the philosophies and approaches of Indian Affairs and the Secretary of State widened. In 1974 the program came under the exclusive mandate of the Department of Indian Affairs, where it has remained to this day.

Unlike other cultural centres across Canada, the cultural educational centres in Ontario became a focal point for a number of thrusts in art programming. The Woodland Indian Cultural Educational Centre at Brantford and the North American Indian Travelling College at Cornwall provided art programs to Indian communities in the south. The Woodland Centre, with a focus on interpretive, educational exhibitions, continues to sponsor an annual art exhibition to showcase new artists and survey any emerging artistic trends. For the north, the Ojibway and Cree Cultural Centre at Timmins and the Ojibwe Cultural Foundation on Manitoulin Island provide a variety of programs specifically designed for artists' development. The latter, under the direction of Mary Lou Fox Radulovich, has become a major centre for artists in a "revitalization" program of traditional Indian culture.

Roz Vanderburgh, an anthropologist with the University of Toronto, noted in her research that this revitalization of the traditional culture by Manitoulin artists was a direct result of combining elders' conferences with summer programs for young artists. Here, in a common forum, elders were able to tell the young artists legends from the past; the artists in turn translated the information into their paintings. Similar experiences had been documented by Morrisseau, Carl Ray, and Daphne Odjig; however, their information sources were in most cases their grandfathers.

This theory of revitalization was also supported by Ruth Phillips and Valda Blundell in a paper they presented in 1982 to the Canadian Ethnology Society. Utilizing art-historical methods, they concluded: "Legend paintings can be regarded as a revival of traditional art forms as well as a redefinition of 'Indianness' in the context of contemporary and multi-cultural Canadian society."

Over the years, support for the visual arts in Ontario also came from a variety of friendship centres. The Native Canadian Centre of Toronto is in the forefront, with its National Indian Art Auction. Others, such as the Nishnawbe Institute in Toronto and Manitoulin, the Association for Native Development in the Visual and Performing Arts in Toronto, and the Manitou Arts Foundation on Schreiber Island have been instrumental in the evolutionary process towards the new art. Dr. Bernhard Cinader, an immunologist and an avid collector, asserts that the activities of the Manitou Arts Foundation were an influential factor in establishing the direction of the art program at the Ojibwe Cultural Foundation.

From 1969 through to the end of the seventies, the White Paper influenced any negotiations between the Indian political associations and government. It was a period of strained relationships. Indian politicians generally maintained a hands-off approach to specific Indian Affairs cultural programs, such as the marketing and promotion of Indian arts and crafts, the cultural education centres, and the cultural affairs program, with its curatorial responsibility for the departmental collection. Much of their attention was focussed on social and political issues — land claims, Indian Act revisions, Indian control of Indian education, and economic development. Indian artists generally had to fend for themselves.

In October 1978 the first Native Artist Conference was held on Manitoulin Island. The conference provided an opportunity for Indian artists to take a retrospective look at the past two decades of programs and influences that had affected them. A number of representatives from cultural institutions and government agencies were also in attendance. Some of the discussion groups exploded into confrontations between the officials and the artists, when conceptions and misconceptions that institutions had harboured towards Indian art were challenged. It became apparent that Indian art had still not attained the status of genuine art among the Canadian art establishment. Alex Janvier, one of the more vocal Indian artists at the conference, commented:

> It is obvious from my view that these organizations we have come across are of little value or are of no use to us. It seems that they have their priorities and are engaged in something a little different than what we are. I think we have a commitment to ourselves as artists, to our tribes and to Indian people in general.

What is clear is that some Indian artists will continue to produce work reflecting the realities of their human condition, which happens to be Indian. Is it this sense of "Indian consciousness," which permeates even the most modern canvases, that inhibits Indian art's credibility for an art gallery, relegating the work to an anthropological museum? If so, the Indian artist is not going to give up his perception of his community just to gain entrance to the art establishment.

The battle still rages. At the third Native Artist Conference at Hazelton, B.C., in August 1983, most of the same issues were addressed. One of the artists stated that he "felt like a pawn in someone else's game. One day there is a marketing program for you and the next day it closes. One year you're worshipped, the next year you're ignored."

Over the past twenty years, the Indian artists of the new art have encountered myriad Indian and non-Indian institutions, each desiring to give economic and intellectual credibility to Native art. For Morrisseau and the image makers, market credibility has been proven; intellectual credibility is forthcoming, but the politics have been awesome.

The Emergence of the Image Makers
Elizabeth McLuhan

1 Norval Morrisseau: Bridging Two Cultures

This book is a visual journey following one man's search for a style that would bridge two cultures, a style that could communicate the essence of Ojibwa values and perceptions to contemporary Native and non-Native viewers alike. In the course of his career, or spirit quest, Norval Morrisseau's work has evolved, as have his own beliefs and paths of self-knowledge. He has been joined on his journey by other artists also concerned with redefining their Indianness and with transmitting Indian culture to new generations. In this book we examine their particular style, but do not do full justice to any single artist.

Although contemporary Canadian Indian artists share no single style, they share the common purpose of reconstituting a holistic vision of the world. Their diversity reflects the personal and selective melding of Indian traditions and twentieth-century international art. The pictographic style of painting originated by Norval Morrisseau and practised by other Cree-Ojibwa-Odawa artists of Ontario can be traced back to its Indian roots, and has clear formal and iconographic parameters that encompass a whole range of artists. Its "Indian-ness" has nothing to do with ethnic authenticity, which has no bearing on the value of the art; rather, examination of the traditional sources of contemporary Indian art conveys the full extent of the non-European system of thought expressed by the style, a system through which even the white presence is incorporated into a non-historical or mythic framework.

The rudiments of pictographic painting – the expressive formline, the system of transparency, of interconnecting lines that determine relationships in terms of spiritual power – were in place in Morrisseau's work by 1963. The Ojibwa cosmology emerged in all its complexity. At the centre was always the image of the artist changing, vascillating between two worlds, caught between cultures. Ojibwa wisdom had traditionally addressed the perennial issues of survival and death, of continuity and adaptation in a harsh environment. The old stories of the forces of nature provided a powerful allegory for the contemporary forces of a white-controlled Indian destiny. Shamans were no longer acknowl-edged or welcomed in the now-Christianized Indian communities, where image making was suspect all the more for being from a primitive past. But an artist commanded respect in the white world. The images were strong medicine.

The pictographic style spoke directly to viewers, with an intense subjectivity, from a world view that was distinctively not Euro-Canadian but Ojibwa. It was neither a sentimental nor nostalgic view but one of enduring spiritual values. And yet Morrisseau's personal search for identity appealed to the Canadian (non-Indian) public of the sixties, and to a country in search of a culturally distinctive national identity. Paradoxically, most Indian communities were attempting to shed their Indianness at this time and to assume a white veneer.

The pictographic style addresses Indian and non-Indian viewers, and could only have been created in this contemporary context. Sacred pictography was utilized traditionally as a system of symbolic communication, abbreviated signs that charted spiritual development and expressed spiritual identity within a larger cosmology. Today, it is an art of violent social change and cultural metamorphosis, of the need for ritual and spiritual connection, of survival in a threatened and threatening environment. It is the art of human odyssey.

Morrisseau, an Ojibwa from northwestern Ontario, invented and continues to refine the style. Carl Ray, a Cree from Sandy Lake, adapted the style to an illustrative mode, adhering closely to legends and events for subject matter. The combined impact of Morrisseau and Ray fostered an entire generation of young Indian artists in northwestern Ontario, including numerous painters in Sandy Lake alone. Of these northwestern protégés, Joshim Kakegamic, Saul Williams, and Roy Thomas represent a maturing of the second generation of Indian artists. These artists have worked primarily or exclusively in the pictographic style and have extended its formal possibilities in new directions. The result has been a northwestern Ontario regional school of preferred colours and line.

Daphne Odjig, an Odawa from Manitoulin Island, brought to the style a fluid line and rich texture. Odjig's long career extends geographically from Wikwemikong, Ontario, to Winnipeg and Vancouver. Few Indian artists have been so formally or consciously innovative as Odjig. Carl Ray and Daphne Odjig approached Morriseau's pictographic style as a vehicle for doing or saying certain things that could not be conveyed in the styles they already employed. Both artists had worked in representational or illustrative modes. Odjig had established a reputation for depicting scenes from life on the reserve; Ray produced frequently garish and nostalgic landscapes of northern Ontario. Both proved that the pictographic style could be adapted and personalized by others.

Blake Debassige epitomizes a generation of younger artists nurtured by the older artists and instructors of the Manitou Arts Foundation on Schreiber Island in 1971-73, and the later Native-run Ojibwe Cultural Foundation in West Bay, Manitoulin Island. Their art records and transmits Native knowledge and values to Native viewers while being *bought* by white patrons. To accomplish the teaching task, the artists discovered that greater self-knowledge and study with Indian elders was required. The Ojibwe Cultural Foundation's extensive work with elders did much to reopen the traditional channels of learning. Debassige and the other artists of Manitoulin Island who work in this pictographic style also express formal preferences for long spidery lines, blended colours, and sophisticated textures that define a regional school distinct from their second-generation counterparts in northwestern Ontario.

From its inception the pictographic style has been alternately referred to as "Woodland Indian art," "legend painting," or "x-ray art" – labels striving for anthropological validation, terms unsuited to convey the aesthetic intent and inventiveness of the art and its reciprocal relationship with the Canadian art market. A dual consciousness pervades the style, which was aptly designed to update and interpret contemporary Indian thought and values to non-Indians and later to Indians themselves. At its best the style is revisionist, rewriting Indian history from an Indian perspective. Badly done, the style degenerates to simply another stereotype, such as the legend mentality, for example. Pictographic painters broke through the pan-Indian generic label to give "Ojibwa," "Odawa," and "Cree" a look and distinctiveness different from west-coast totem poles and Plains Indian headdresses. They speak as individuals and as professional artists about identity and survival.

THE PRE-PICTOGRAPHIC PHASE

In tracing the invention of the pictographic style, it is necessary to focus almost exclusively on Norval Morrisseau from 1958 to 1965. During those years he adapted and synthesized enormous amounts of information on materials, techniques, art history, and the white art market. In the late 1960s he was joined by other artists.

Norval Morrisseau was born in 1932 in Sand Point Reserve (which was "cancelled" in the fifties), on Lake Nipigon, near Thunder Bay. He was most nurtured by his maternal grandparents, particularly Moses "Potan" Nana-konagos. It was through his grandfather that he received a mission to transmit, through his art, the legacy of Ojibwa values and beliefs to Indians and non-Indians. For a young man who lived in the remote small town of Beardmore and who left school at grade four, the opportunity for exposure to the visual arts was almost nonexistent. According to Herbert Schwarz in *Windigo and Other Tales of the Ojibways*, which Morrisseau illustrated, like many Indians Morrisseau would "pick up some magazines and comics thrown out by the white man." The fact that the artist and his family lived near the garbage dump makes an apocryphal image, for Norval became an archaeologist of white culture, excavating information from its refuse in a community that was itself an outpost of Canadian life. What he found vital and immediate, however, were the Ojibwa teachings, the elders' knowledge, the rock paintings by unknown predecessors, and the tools of shamanism and the Midewiwin medico-religious society. The Ojibwa oral tradition, the mnemonic pictography or memory aids, and the decorative arts provided a rich environment of form and imagery. Although suffering the ravages of poverty, illness, and alcoholism, Morrisseau became an avid student of his culture and was a proficient craftsman himself. As James Stevens has pointed out in an unpublished manuscript, "Many refer only to Norval's problems with alcohol and forget he is an accomplished man in several endeavours. He is a ma-mandowininih [or] a medicine man . . . a basketmaker, a carver of spoons and statues, an eloquent singer of Indian medicine songs and an unrivalled raconteur of legends and humorous stories."

A succession of formative relationships with doctors, arts professionals, teachers, and patrons accelerated his stylistic development. The first acknowledged supporter was Dr. Henry Weinstein, who provided Morrisseau with art materials and access to his art history library in Red Lake, where Morrisseau had moved in 1959 to work in the gold mines. Selwyn Dewdney, an early colleague of and literary collaborator with Morrisseau, met the artist in 1960 through a local OPP constable, Robert Sheppard, on MacKenzie Island, near Red Lake. He recounts a fascinating story, in "Birth of a Cree-Ojibwa Style of Contemporary Art," of trying to determine just which books in Weinstein's library of non-Western or "pre-literate art" could appeal to Morrisseau most.

> A day or two later [in 1960] Norval and I were invited to the Weinsteins' for supper. I asked Norval to pick out the books of reproductions that had interested him most. Without hesitation he selected two: one of Navajo art, the other of West Coast painting and sculpture. Yet scanning the contents of either to compare them to Morrisseau's work in the same room, it was clear to me that although there were a few instances where subjects coincided, the styles were poles apart.

Only later did Dewdney have the chance to become familiar with Ontario Shield rock paintings and the Midewiwin scrolls, which were the sources of Morrisseau's paintings.

Morrisseau met his wife, Harriet Kakegamic, while being hospitalized for tuberculosis in Fort William (now Thunder Bay) from 1956-57. Harriet, who

1
Norval Morrisseau
Man Changing into Thunderbird c.1958-60
Tempera on birch bark
63.0 x 101.3 cm
National Museum of Man, Ottawa

hailed from Sandy Lake, returned to Beardmore with Norval upon his release. Soon with a family to support, Morrisseau turned to painting in a more serious way from 1958 on.

In works dating from 1958 to 1960, Morrisseau set out the themes and concerns he would deal with for the next twenty years. In *Man Changing into Thunderbird* of 1958-60 (No. I), Morrisseau established a life-long theme of the self and transformation, of the many levels of human (and therefore spiritual) existence. In effecting a cure for his illness, a medicine woman had bestowed the name Copper Thunderbird upon the artist in his youth in 1948. The painting could be viewed as one of his earliest self-portraits. Although employing the "Indian" medium of birch bark and pan-Indian symbols, the work is awkward and stiff. Western pictorial conventions of clothing and naturalistic details of the eagle collide with the geometric references to Indian design in the bird wings. Already there is a foreshadowing of stylistic change in the self-conscious use of zigzag emanating lines, empty and divided circles, and dots, which transcend the decorative speckle effect to designate special power on the pendant medicine pouch around the eagle's neck.

Medicine Snake Motif of 1958-60 (No. 2) achieves a rough mosaic effect of geometric patterns. Horns crown the serpent heads and the long divided tongues are curled to echo the curved ridges on the snake's back, which culminates in a split tail. Once again a double entity is portrayed. The serpent, which in the earlier *Man Changing into Thunderbird* (No. 1) is clutched in the eagle's claws, is here let loose in one of the first of many reincarnations to follow. The double outlines and segmented innards create the impression of an applied quill or bead design. The snake was to evolve as a potent symbol of human passion in Morrisseau's later work – a force constantly at odds with his spiritual development.

In the untitled work on birch bark of the same period (No. 3, colour plate p. 33), depicting the shaking-tent ceremony, Morrisseau's archetypal figures are clothed in more simplified and ceremonial attire. This is one of the first of many depictions of ancestral figures. The image is nonetheless awkward, with its mask-like profiled faces, and noses and mouths like an afterthought. Naturalistic detail has been minimized for greater effect, even to the extent of fingerless hands. Two lower circles echo the shape of the drum in the hands of the figure of the left. The arc in the upper middle picture depicts a domed, bark-covered shaking tent – a visual pun, since the painting medium itself is birch bark. The seams of the hut may also be seen as energy lines with secondary bristles. These timeless figures in a mythical landscape later became idealized self-portraits, imagined predecessors, and Indianized Christian saints.

Morrisseau's use of bark for painting has several explanations. As Stevens points out, Morrisseau was a craftsman who worked in the medium. Bark was an "acceptably Indian" medium for public sale. The Midewiwin scrolls were made of bark. And most importantly of all, bark cost nothing but the effort to gather and prepare it. Ironically this early work on bark, painted in a hodgepodge mixture of watercolours, oils, and inks, is more derivative of Western painting conventions than his later work. From 1958 to 1960 works were executed on any medium available, including plywood, hide, and kraft paper, in crayon, oils, and probably anything at hand.

THE SECULARIZATION OF OJIBWA PICTOGRAPHY

Although much has been made of Morrisseau's self-taught status and lack of education, early in his teens he rejected European formal modes of learning and actively sought to acquire traditional Ojibwa knowledge and values. While the public marvelled, after his first commercial exhibit in Toronto in 1962, that an

3
Norval Morrisseau
Untitled c. 1958-61
Tempera on birch bark
90.0 x 68.8 cm
National Museum of Man, Ottawa

5
Norval Morrisseau
Serpent Legend c. 1961
Tempera and ink on card
78.7 x l06.7 cm
Collection of Dr. Bernhard Cinader, F.R.C.S.,
   Toronto

12
Norval Morrisseau
Portrait of the Artist as Jesus Christ 1966
Acrylic on kraft paper
184.5 x 91.9 cm
Guardian Capital Group, Limited, Art Collection

16
Norval Morrisseau
Joseph with Christ Child and St. John the Baptist
    1973
Acrylic on canvas
101.6 x 81.3 cm
Department of Indian and Northern Affairs, Indian
    Art Centre

17
Norval Morrisseau
Virgin Mary with Christ Child and St. John the
    Baptist 1973
Acrylic on canvas
101.6 x 81.3 cm
Department of Indian and Northern Affairs, Indian
    Art Centre

21
Norval Morrisseau
The Story-teller: The Artist and His Grandfather
  1978
Acrylic on canvas
Two panels, each 174.0 x 92.3 cm
Department of Indian and Northern Affairs,
  Indian Art Centre

23
Daphne Odjig
Collage c. 1971
Mixed media
66.0 x 94.0 cm
Dr. H. T. Schwarz, Quebec

18
Norval Morrisseau
Warrior with Thunderbirds 1973
Acrylic on masonite
121.8 x 122.1 cm
Collection of Helen E. Band, Toronto

25
Daphne Odjig
From Mother Earth Flows the River of Life 1973
Acrylic on canvas
153.8 x 215.2 cm
National Museum of Man, Ottawa

29
Carl Ray
Thunderbirds 1972-73
Acrylic on masonite
101.6 x 76.2 cm
The Confederation College of Applied Arts & Tech-
    nology, Thunder Bay

39
Josh Kakegamic
Boy in the Moon 1980
Acrylic on canvas
91.0 x 122.0 cm
National Museum of Man, Ottawa

42
Saul Williams
Medicine Man's Dream of Christ 1973
Acrylic on paper
75.0 x 56.0 cm
Private Collection

40

Roy Thomas

The Eagle Will Fly 1981

Acrylic on canvas

121.0 x 151.5 cm

Woodland Indian Cultural Educational Centre,

  Brantford

48
Blake Debassige
Tree of Life n.d.
Acrylic on canvas
1.2 x 2.4 m
Anishnabe Spiritual Centre, Espanola, Ontario

47
Blake Debassige
One Who Lives under the Water 1978
Acrylic on canvas
127.0 x 96.5 cm
Royal Ontario Museum, Toronto

artist of such power could hail from the bush, it was precisely because of conditions there that it was possible to collect and assimilate one's own Indian culture. Morrisseau became a learned man and translated his Ojibwa learning into a new visual language that was neither traditionally Ojibwa nor Euro-Canadian. More surprising, it was art.

Morrisseau drew upon Ojibwa pictography and in doing so secularized visual forms employed previously for spiritual purposes. The emergence of an Ojibwa artist, or image maker, marked a departure from the traditional restriction of image making to participants in spiritual rituals; the creation of images was an integral part of these rituals.

Historically, it is known that Ojibwa pictographic records were created for both secular and sacred functions. Secular records were meant to convey information to all and were of a commonly understood idiom. These ranged from maps, messages to travellers, totemic identification, and inscriptions on grave boards to aids in casual story-telling, in which the Ojibwa excelled.

Religious uses included the private dream images of spirit questers, magical-medicinal charms, which aided in the transfer of spiritual power, and bark scrolls for the Midewiwin Society. In the first instance a young spirit quester, through fasting and physical endurance, would seek a personal vision that would provide him with a guardian spirit and a purpose or path in the life ahead of him. If successful, he would make a sort of representation of the guardian spirit, carved or painted, and keep it with him, first wearing it upon his body and later including it in his Midewiwin medicine bag. As Frances Densmore explained in *Chippewa Customs* (1929), this dream symbol might "publish the subject of a dream but give no indication of its significance." It could be taken from him but could not be used against him.

According to Olive Dickason, Norval Morrisseau fasted in his teens under the guidance of his grandfather and received a vision that assured him of protection in his new mission to paint, during the same period when he received his Indian name, Copper Thunderbird. This thunderbird has served as a life-long talisman, and in his art became a visual alter-ego.

The magical-medicinal charms of the Ojibwa were employed for good luck, for assistance in love, for hunting, and for protecting babies in their cradles. They could also be used to harm others. In curing illness, the shaman directed power from his medicine bag into an image that represented the afflicted person or the spirit who was responsible for the illness. In this way, strength and health were injected into the patient. Images were tools of manipulation for good or ill. Morrisseau, trained as a shaman, turned to images to revitalize an ailing Ojibwa culture.

The third application of image making was made by the Midewiwin Society, a medico-religious group of herbalist-healers thought to have originated in historical times. Their bark records were mnemonic devices called "instruction scrolls" by Selwyn Dewdney in *The Sacred Scrolls of the Southern Ojibwa*. According to Frances Densmore, they helped preserve the traditions of the society in both song and ceremonial procedure. W.J. Hoffman explained that they were "a pictorial resume of the traditional history of the origin of the Midewiwin, the positions occupied by the various guardian manidos [manitous] in several degrees, and the order of procedure in the study and progress of the candidate." These records were kept hidden from common view and were unrolled only when a candidate was ready to be advanced. Much like individual dream images, these complex scrolls could be fully explained only by the maker, although the images were generally recognizable by other society members.

There is evidence that Morrisseau was intimately familiar with scroll pictog-

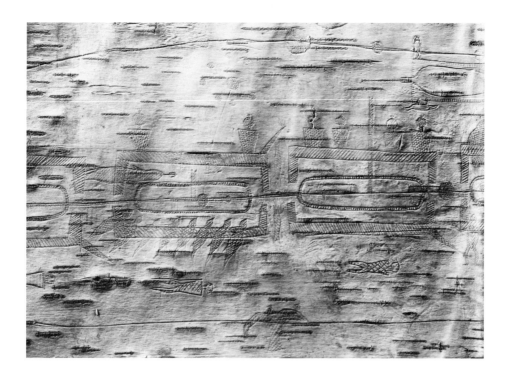

fig. 6 Detail of central motif of Ojibwa birch bark scroll from the Royal Ontario Museum, Toronto; thought to be early twentieth-century.

raphy. In *Coming Away (Legendary Scroll Motifs)* (No. 4), a work executed about 1959, his drawing demonstrates an extraordinary awareness of Native pictography. This work is a "missing link" of sorts – an introduction to the forms and images that would be developed in Morrisseau's work over the next twenty years. It is an artist's reproduction of a scroll – more lineally refined than traditional scrolls, which bore rough figures etched on bark – and yet it shows only a glimpse of the draughtsmanship and painterliness that was to emerge later. By this time Morrisseau was signing his name "Copper Thunderbird" in his own language in syllabics, the first Indian artist to do so; he had been taught Cree syllabics by his wife, Harriet. Both the pictographic images and syllabic signature create a distinctive personal *and* tribal-looking style.

The Midewiwin scrolls were made of bark and the images were etched on the surface with bone or stone tools. As a result the "drawing" was sketchy and awkward. Lines were frequently doubled and filled in with hatching or crosshatching, which made them more readable and created a textured effect similar to that of applied quillwork. These etchings were closer to braille than to painting. As in peeled bark or bitten bark designs, the scroll pictography was created by a process of subtraction to create the images. The overall effect of a classic Midewiwin scroll – as in the example from the Royal Ontario Museum (fig. 6) – was that of finely wrought latticework.

The key to reading these scrolls lies in the combinations of symbols and "determinatives," as W.J. Hoffman aptly termed the connecting lines almost a century ago. These emanating lines define or determine a cosmological status by expressing internal spiritual power and interrelationships. He went on to say, in his early study of the Midewiwin, that "the Ojibwa . . . exhibit greater advancement in the incorporation of gestures and the suggestion of abstract ideas in connection with graphic devices" than other North American Indian cultures.

A Midewiwin scroll was both an architectural blueprint of the ceremonial longhouse and a procedural outline parallelling the lodge's symbolic and actual construction. This architectural/procedural model was also a cosmological chart of Cree-Ojibwa religion. Represented were the archetypal spiritual journey or path of the initiate, and the possible pitfalls and forces of good and evil that

2
Norval Morrisseau
Medicine Snake Motif c.1958-60
Wax crayon on brown paper
71.7 x 81.0 cm
National Museum of Man, Ottawa

4
Norval Morrisseau
Coming Away (Legendary Scroll Motifs) c.1959
Ink on paper
6l.6 x 122.2 cm
Collection of Helen E. Band, Toronto

the initiate would have to face. Featured in the scrolls was a cast of supernatural manitous, Midewiwin priests and representatives, and the initiate himself. Through the enactment of the Midewiwin ritual spiritual passages were marked, certain beliefs were renewed, and knowledge was passed on.

Although it would be fruitless to attempt to decode specific meanings in the pictography, a visual system did exist to communicate to others within the community. Scrolls and records continue to be passed on – and to find their way to museums. As E.S. Rogers has pointed out, traditional shamanism has mutated into a suspect form of black magic or Christian evangelism in some communities. Reserves have been missionized, and they profess Christianity in all its various sects. For an avid Indian student of traditional non-Christian ways, information about old ways can be secured perhaps through a grandfather and other elders who realize that the oral traditions, with the language, are slipping away. There are also the ageless rock paintings – "the Indians' cathedrals" as Morrisseau called them – to be marvelled at. Morrisseau himself received training as a shaman, and James Stevens reports that for awhile the artist practised his vocation. He brings this training to bear in his role as an artist, through his knowledge of traditional pictography and his overwhelming concern with spiritual health and growth.

Midewiwin pictography documented and facilitated the transfer of spiritual power. Sacred power or spiritual attributes were denoted by lines emanating from designated figures. These lines could be straight or wavy. Meanings were derived from the path of the lines. Lines connecting two or more figures expressed power relationships or sensory links. The network of "determinative" lines greatly amplified the range of expression, defined relationships more precisely, and compressed alot of information into the limited space of the scrolls. According to Hoffman, "the figures are more than simply mnemonic: they are ideographic and frequently possess additional interest from the fact that several ideas are expressed in combination." Almost ninety years later, Dewdney summarized some of the characteristics of scroll pictography as "rectilinear . . . abstraction . . . elaboration . . . symbol conversion . . . condensation."

A scroll was horizontal and rectangular, as was the Midewiwin lodge depicted. Since the nineteenth century the long bark records were stored rolled up. Pieces could be added or sewed on. The scrolls were etched, not painted, and the designs almost imperceptible unless looked for. Degrees or grades in the society were depicted as successive lozenge-shaped lodges. Human figures were often decorative rows of heads and torsos. Animal and human figures frequently bore cross-hatched filler. They were abstracted to their most typical forms and gestures. Stick-figure humans were usually portrayed frontally, with gangly limbs. Horns or other attributes indicated actual physical qualities or super-human identities. Turtle-manitous were outlined in overview, emphasizing the shell. Profiled bear-manitous were drawn with jaws agape and massive trunk. Combinations of emanating lines, clusters of dots, or atypical horns acknowledged the varying degrees of spiritual power of the figures they described.

The system of expressive internal parts, frequently mislabelled "x-ray," was a spiritual gauge of the figure portrayed and a description of his relationship to the outer world. A line extending from the mouth through the throat to a circular or ovoid form in the chest represented the life line attached to the heart, or the life force itself. The "heart" could be outsized to indicate a fullness of spirit, or an attribute such as bravery.

Circles and ovoids recurred with many variations. Dewdney traces the prototype to the megis shell, a salt-water shell similar to a cowry, ovoid and

fig. 7 A copy of a rock painting at Agawa Canyon. The copy is by Selwyn Dewdney and appears in *Indian Rock Paintings of the Great Lakes*.

folded inwards to form two halves. The megis was an important part of Midewiwin medicine bag and was a source of a shaman's power. It was with the medicine bag that the shaman "shot" health or spiritual assistance into images.

Scrolls were created by and for Midewiwin Society members, both men and women. As Hoffman indicates, although scroll pictography was elaborate it was not codified, and could be interpreted accurately only by its author. A single scroll with a single author/interpreter could have several meanings. Dewdney explains that "a Mide master was free to make selections from the total lore at his command, producing simple condensed accounts for one purpose or relating in detail one or more variations on the same theme, some of which, taken literally, contradict each other."

Although of undetermined origin, the rock paintings (fig. 7) found in abundance in the Great Lakes and Canadian Shield region bear a remarkable similarity to the vocabulary of form in Ojibwa scroll pictography. Figures portrayed range from identifiable game animals and human beings to ambiguous geometric symbols and more recent graffiti. Side by side is a class of fantasy or hybrid creations noted by Selwyn Dewdney and Kenneth Kidd, composites of symbols or creatures. The exact age of the rock paintings cannot be determined. Nancy-Lou Patterson estimates that some are over a thousand years old, judging from the plant overgrowth. These rock faces are accessible to an artist in a canoe, and at some sites there are ledges upon which to balance, according to Zenon Poherecky.

As a form of expression, rock paintings are less accessible and less explicable than the pictography of the scrolls. They were painted rather than etched – and made to last and to communicate. Dewdney and Kidd point out that "there is strong evidence in the Shield paintings of an interest in content that almost constantly overrides the interest in form." These paintings are generally thought to have been made by spirit questers and medicine men. Even today visitors leave small offerings on nearby ledges in the less remote locations.

Pictography used for secular purposes was not concerned with the transfer of power but rather with general information or decoration. Although secular pictography bore a general resemblance to the sacred in its vocabulary of form,

fig. 8 Late-nineteenth-century Eastern Woodland (probably Ojibwa) birch bark container from the Royal Ontario Museum, Toronto.

the system of linear notations or spiritual determinatives was not employed. In a trapezoidal container with peeled-bark design from Ontario (fig. 8), it is possible to recognize the stratified human and deer figures enclosed by zigzag and saw-toothed frames. Figures are silhouetted and in motion in typical or recognizable gestures. No lines connect the figures or define their spiritual attributes.

Looking again at Morrisseau's *Coming Away (Legendary Scroll Motifs)* (No. 4), the most notable difference from traditional pictography is its execution with ink on paper. Many figures are recognizable, although altered by horns or emanating lines – bears, turtles, fish, serpents, mermen, birds, humans. Lodges house supernatural participants. There are only the most cursory references to landscape. Cross-hatching has been carried over to emphasize certain double lines and to fill in the torsos of several figures. A complex network of lines interconnects all the pictorial elements. These lines serve virtually every function – descriptive outlines, lines of movement as in the shaking tent at upper left, lines from the senses, life lines, horns of power, and lines that seem simply to resonate with energy. While the pictorial space is filled, it is not unified nor is the image plane structured. This drawing is an important work in its establishment of Morrisseau's early knowledge of pictography and in the introduction of the entire cast of characters and formal conventions that would follow in his art. But it is clearly experimental.

In 1960 and 1962, Morrisseau gave Selwyn Dewdney two manuscripts, which became the basis for a collaboration and finally a book, *Legends of My People, The Great Ojibway*, published in 1965. The book was edited and organized into themes or stories and used Morrisseau's paintings from that period, reproduced in black-and-white, as illustrations. What's more, Jack Pollock met Morrisseau independently and had effectively launched his career with a commercial art exhibit in Toronto in 1962. The transition had been made from shaman to artist.

Works executed between 1960 and 1963 clearly illustrate Morrisseau's successful adaptation of pictography to a painterly mode. In the 1961 *Serpent Legend* (No. 5, colour plate p. 34) the powerful calligraphic line asserts itself. The artist has structured and unified the image plane. The horned serpent turns inward to contain three human figures and meets the fourth to transact a power transfer from his horn through the other's puckered mouth and beak-like nose. The figure's single ponytail of flowing hair could be a double reference to the power being acquired by the medicine man. The circle-and-dot eyes are echoed by the circled syllabic signature or "I" of the artist. Torsos follow the scroll conventions; the artist has retained the cross-hatching but added hieroglyphic-looking designs to fill the serpent's body; and with the horns, bristles, and emanating lines, he establishes its supernatural authority. Morrisseau has reduced his colour palette to black, brown, and white, achieving a sense of primitiveness through the non-traditional media of ink, tempera, and acrylics on kraft paper.

Morrisseau instinctively clothed and amplified the pictographic vocabulary of form and restructured this image bank into a powerful art expression. The Ojibwa pictographic system provided him with building blocks. But the final invention was his own. During the period 1960 to 1963 one can sense the artist stepping back, and starting again; for while works from the preceding period employ a wide colour palette along with Western conventions of representation, his studies from this period favour black and brown primary and secondary contour lines on white, neutral, or construction-paper backgrounds.

Thunderbird Man of 1962 (No. 6) provides a fascinating counterpoint to

Morrisseau's earlier depiction on birch bark of *Man Changing into Thunderbird*. The image is a model of streamlined compactness. In a single figure he has depicted the inextricable duality of this man/bird. In brown and black oils on a white watercolour paper, Morrisseau portrays the double identity as a costumed figure. The head and wing of an eagle are worn like a hood and mantle over the torso of a man. One of the legs is stained brown like the other eagle wing and culminates in feather and talons. Clothing is abstracted to suggestions of mukluk, waistband, and shirt.

These linear references may double as the hieroglyphic filler seen in *Serpent Legend* (No. 5). Once again the torso is frontal and the head profiled. This time the artist has balanced the weight of the wing on the upper left, with the bird's leg on the lower right. The wing is segmented but a single colour and shared linear filler maintain the visual unity. As in the painting on bark, the eye itself is a divided circle. Here, it constitutes almost the entire head. The beak has been left open – and its teeth transform the beak to animal jaws. In place of a pendant medicine bag in the earlier work, there is a divided ovoid, perhaps a medicine bag or the very "heart" of the figure. The recognizable human attributes such as the arm are simplified, tapering to a point. The internal parts of the human side contain segmented circles radiating somewhat regimented hooked lines. The artist has signed his name under the human foot. In *Thunderbird Man* and *Serpent Legend*, Morrisseau's formline has become strong, individualistic, and calligraphic in its undulating movement, its swelling and contracting. The formline is enhanced by secondary lines, usually brown, and by a third colour for filler. On brown kraft paper, this tertiary colour is frequently white.

THE ICONIC PICTOGRAPHIC PHASE

Following Morrisseau's first Toronto show, a subsequent exhibit was held at the Pollock Gallery in 1963, but received little attention. It was not until 1972 that he had another major commercial exhibit in that city. Consequently, much of his work during this period was not generally known as it evolved.

Between 1963 and 1966, however, Morrisseau's painting achieved a maturing of form and line, a richness of colour, and a daring breakthrough in sheer scale. Images from this period convey such a timeless power and such a sense of definitive archetypal form that they deserve the term "icon."

Sacred White Bear (No. 7) depicts with every linear device the benign but powerful aspect of the bear, a creature said to have once had human form. There are horns, emanating lines, divided circles, the pendant medicine bag, an internal life line, and dot clusters on feet and ankles. The divided circles are possessed of internal bristling lines and resonate with energy to and from the bear. The colour white amplifies the albino bear's power. Work portraying cosmological figures has been dubbed "legend painting," but in fact Morrisseau's work has never been strictly descriptive or narrative. As in *Sacred White Bear*, images convey essences more than actions. Given the traditional multiple levels of meaning of pictography, any single "legend" interpretation of the painting constricts the artist's intent. Published books, whether written by Indians and/or non-Indians, document and preserve some sense of Indian oral traditions but distort them simultaneously by the literal single version affixed to each image. Traditionally a story would change with each telling, and an image would offer new perception with each viewing, depending on the context.

Two books, *Legends of My People, The Great Ojibway*, edited by Selwyn Dewdney, and *Windigo and Other Tales of the Ojibways* of 1969, by Herbert Schwarz, both use paintings by Morrisseau as illustrations and provide a study in contrasts. In the first, Morrisseau's voice remains distinctive and the "legends"

6
Norval Morrisseau
Thunderbird Man c.1962
Oil on watercolour paper
70.5 x 46.0 cm
Collection of Susan A. Ross, Thunder Bay

7
Norval Morrisseau
Sacred White Bear n.d.
Tempera on brown building paper
76.2 x 121.9 cm
Glenbow Museum, Calgary, Alberta

8
Norval Morrisseau
Windigo c. 1964
Tempera on brown building paper
157.5 x 81.3 cm
Glenbow Museum, Calgary, Alberta

9
Norval Morrisseau
Indian Vision: Woman c.1964
Tempera on brown building paper
157.5 x 81.3 cm
Glenbow Museum, Calgary, Alberta

10
Norval Morrisseau
Indian Vision: Man c.1964
Tempera on brown building paper
159.0 x 81.3 cm
Glenbow Museum, Calgary, Alberta

are a spicy combination of anecdotes, history, healing remedies, humour, cultural commentary, violence, and warnings. The latter book is a series of discreet short stories in the Western tradition. The many other books to follow between 1969 and 1972, with white narrators and Indian paintings as illustration, popularly characterized Indian artists as mere story-tellers. And yet, even when a painting by Morrisseau features characters from Ojibwa history or traditions, the image does not tell a story but rather describes spiritual power struggles and gauges the balance between good and evil. Viewer interest derives from the power of the imagery to draw one into a larger holistic world view.

In No. 8, *Windigo* (c. 1964), perhaps the most literal of his paintings, a huge humanoid monster devours beavers that are, in fact, human beings. The power in the white hair gone wild, the saw-toothed mouth, and the dead lump of a heart convey a duality, a good gone bad. The wide eye seems to weep ice and the usually divided resonating circle of energy in front of his face is empty. There is a horizon line of tipis, lodges, and stretched pelts that provides a scale for the Windigo's towering size. The village is reminiscent of the rendering in *Untitled* (No. 3), but the contour line is surer, more expressive, and the figure free of any naturalistic constrictions. *Windigo* embodies human fear, the spectre of madness and the horror of cannibalism – the dualities of human nature. As John Robert Colombo explains in his anthology on the subject, this fear is a spectre none escape. Morrisseau's *Windigo* is all the more powerful in its crudeness. The white paint is thickly and unevenly applied in daubs on the Windigo's body, along the horizon line, and more simply at the sides of the creature, as though he were shedding or moulting his outer veneer of civilization. This shocking glimpse of man's dark side was created in the same period as *Sacred White Bear* (No. 7), a painting of control and equilibrium.

The companion pieces, *Indian Vision: Woman* and *Indian Vision: Man* (Nos. 9, 10) of about 1964, are a dramatic departure in concept and execution: a two-panel idealization of the artist and his wife in heaven. The figures are costumed in robes and headdresses evocative of Northwest Coast Indian regalia, recalling Dewdney's comments about Morrisseau's early interest in Northwest Coast Indian art books. On closer examination, individual elements such as the totemic figure on the woman's dress, the similarity of the man's cape to a button blanket, and the headdresses like upturned war canoes seem individually derivative, but the overall effect is totally original. Comparing the *Indian Vision: Man* to his painting on birch bark *Man Changing into Thunderbird* (No. 1), the similarities are overwhelming, particularly the stance of both figures. The earlier wing has been replaced by the cape, and the figure still wears mukluks. Lines at the waist, neck, and arm have been elaborated upon with decorative paraphernalia. The pendant necklace of *Indian Vision: Man* echoes the shape of the heart – and multiplies it.

With the creation of the two *Indian Vision* pieces several things occur. The earlier images of ancestor figures have been reincarnated as a visionary self-portrait and portrait of his wife. The declamatory images of Copper Thunderbird have become personal dream images, states of the self, levels to be attained, a journal of the spirit's journey. Morrisseau's images express both the Midewiwin Society's concern for the correct path of life and a spirit quester's search for a talisman or protective image. According to Basil Johnston in *Ojibway Heritage*:

> For the Anishnabe the vision became the theme and quest in his life that attained the character of force; as a force, it could alter the course of individuals, bend the nature of living, enhance the tone of the life, and change character....For with the coming of vision, existence became living...so man in receiving a vision had to live it out.

11
Norval Morrisseau
Man and Snake c. 1965
Tempera on brown building paper
175.9 x 81.3 cm
Glenbow Museum, Calgary, Alberta

Morrisseau's paintings document one man's spirit quest, and in a departure from Indian traditions he made them public. These images are portraits of the inner self, of the dream, and later of the torment.

Man and Snake (No. 11) of 1965 is one of the earliest works dealing with the theme of inner battles and conflicting dualities. The medicine snake has become a many-headed serpent of temptation, a creature of Christianity, not of the Midewiwin. The human figure is clothed in snakes like some perverse personal adornment. Stripped bare to the waist, the figure wears trousers out of which crawls another phallic serpent head. The artist has written of the image, "Any man who is attached to sence's (sic) and desires and richs (sic) of this world is like a man who is being devoured by serpents who represents (sic) his own passion and desires." The intensity and passion of the picture declare it a self-portrait. Such confessionalism, brutal, direct, and unapologetic, was unprecedented in the Indian community and beyond the bounds of a colourful story-teller for white viewers.

The iconic pictographic phase saw the emergence of larger, more colourful works and the injection of an intensely individual visionary quality into human figures. As colour was added, the use of linear determinatives lessened. Ancestral portraits proliferated at this time, equal in their rich mosaic quality to *Indian Vision: Man* and *Indian Vision: Woman*. These figures are usually on empty backgrounds, with no visual context at all. The dynamic of the image is contained in the surface design of the costume, which enhances through colour the lines of energy and power. The costumes, the headdresses, the hairdos, are all the creation of the artist to evoke a sense of history and continuity. The rich primary colours, multiple outlines, and segmented surface areas of the costume are akin to the curvilinear beadwork designs of northwestern Ontario. The exploration of colour is tentative, but would be fully developed in later works. The costumes are the first in a long line of imagined ancestral designs.

NATIVE-CHRISTIAN DICHOTOMIES

In *Portrait of the Artist as Jesus Christ* of 1966 (No. 12, colour plate p. 35), the artist has laid claim to the ultimate white ancestral figure and integrated him into a self-portrait of the artist with a mission. The red-hooded figure is a descendant of Morrisseau's earliest ancestor figures on birch bark. The artist/Christ is depicted carrying two medicine bags and wearing around his neck a pendant with the emblem of the cross. Within this cross, however, is the familiar circle and dotted centre; a dotted halo functions as a symbol of power. This is not the conventional image of the artist suffering as Christ. It is a claim by the artist to the power of Christ. It is an amalgam of Christ's status as a shaman and the artist's role as an image maker. It is a challenge thrown back to white missionaries that Christianity may superimpose itself upon Indian culture, but that it cannot supplant Indian religion and identity. The good Christian becomes another persona assumed by the Indian for survival.

The period from 1966 to 1975 was a tumultuous time for the artist. He was invited in 1966 to work on a major mural for the Indians of Canada Pavilion at Expo '67 in Montreal. By that time his work had been acknowledged in a national context but his life had become more violent. Carl Ray, his apprentice, was left to execute much of the work at Expo while Morrisseau embarked on ever more frequent alcoholic binges. Following Expo, he travelled back and forth between Montreal and Vancouver. In 1972 he survived a hotel room fire, receiving burns all over his body except for his hands and face. By 1973 he was in Kenora, where he was jailed for six months, as much for self-protection as for transgressing the law. During this time he started painting in an adjacent cell rigged up as a studio. Works produced were extraordinarily Christian, alternat-

ing with the usual Native images. The police allowed him occasional forays into the community to visit the many Christian churches.

It is possible to trace Morrisseau's increasing cultural schizophrenia through his work. During these years his painting expressed a concern with reconciling Native and Christian imagery and forms. Up to the mid-sixties much of his work drew consciously from Native sources, both pictography and the decorative arts. The images were aggressively Indian. But with the emergence of self-portraits came the dilemma of how one was defined and by whom.

Floral Still Life of 1969-70 (No. 13) is a strange combination of Western and Indian conventions. The more he experimented with European forms the more an Ojibwa sensibility came to the fore. While the flowers sprout from what appears to be a bark planter, they retain the colour and structure of Ojibwa applied beadwork – as can be seen by comparing this to the beaded bag of 1929 from Red Lake (fig. 9). They share a preference for a monochrome background, multiple outlines, for blues, reds, pinks, greens, and yellows, and the extension of the floral design to fill any given space. During this period he also rendered the familiar loon and fish imagery into almost unrecognizable layers of roughly applied paint, testing the limits of the style to the point that the images were obscured by the paint itself.

In 1972 he was converted to the Apostolic faith and much of the art of this period deals with his conversion. Paradoxically, Morrisseau was creating some of his most graphically realized Indian images shortly before and after his conversion. *Riding the Thunderbird* of 1972 (No. 14) and *Water Spirit* (No. 15) of the same year are dramatic counterpoints to the Christian images in their linear power and movement. Colour is secondary to line, reduced to filler. The linear determinatives surround and unify the picture. The shaman is once again let loose to control the powers of the thunderbird. The image is a balance of power unleashed and power constrained. The four divided circles are echoed in the pendants around the shaman's neck, in the markings of the thunderbird's tail and feathers, the eyes of man and birds, and the divided ovoids in the birds' chests.

Water Spirit retains the curvilinear silhouette of the Agawa rocking painting

13
Norval Morrisseau
Floral Still Life 1969-70
Acrylic on paper
40.6 x 70.0 cm
Dr. H. T. Schwarz, Quebec

14
Norval Morrisseau
Riding the Thunderbird 1972
Acrylic on kraft paper
101.6 x 161.3 cm
Department of Indian and Northern Affairs, Indian
   Art Centre

known as the underwater panther (fig. 7). The artist has curled the image back upon itself like a snake eating its tail. Out of the creature's toothed jaw emanates a forked tongue leading to a series of interconnected divided circles that reconnect to the horn on his head. The water spirit is white and filled with dots. The artist has retained the decorative linear hatching that articulates and segments parts of the body.

In two pictures from 1973, *Joseph with Christ Child and St. John the Baptist* and *Virgin Mary with Christ Child and St. John the Baptist* (Nos. 16,17, colour plates pp. 36-37) Morrisseau has Nativized two classic Christian holy card images much as he portrayed the still life gone bush in *Floral Still Life*. The works are perhaps his most tranquil and most still, done while he was drying out in jail. They do not portray the artist-as-Christ challenge, but rather speak to the idea that Christ could have been an Indian. Dubbed the ''stained-glass'' style, they seem to represent a submission to Christianity.

While Morrisseau developed new forms such as the ancestor figures, which later mutated to Christian images, he always retained and continued to perfect his earlier pictographic figures from Indian cosmology. In *Warrior with Thunderbirds* of 1973 (No. 18, colour plate p. 41), Morrisseau integrates the Christian look with Native content in one of his oldest themes, man and thunderbird. The black formline is transformed to a leaded stained-glass effect segmenting the rich blues, reds, browns, greens, and yellows. The warrior is white-haired, his eye repeated in the eyes of his companion birds, and in the designs on their wings. He is enclosed in a bower, protected. It recalls his early vision, recorded by Olive Dickason in *Indian Art in Canada* (1972):

> Morrisseau had a dream, the kind of dream-vision by means of which in the old days young men found their guiding spirits: ''Behind me is a grizzly bear. In front of me two water gods chewing on bones. Something stronger than myself is protecting me from them. Like a shadow. The shadow starts moving. The bear shows his claws. The water gods are coming towards me. I know fear. I run after the shadow. 'Great Spirit! Help me! I am afraid!' It says, 'I'm the Great Manitou. I'm testing you. Now here's a charm for you.' And he throws down two pieces of silk, like flags, yes. Light blue and dark blue. Day sky and night sky. 'These will protect you. Go ahead and do these things. Never fear. I will help you.' Since then I am not afraid.''

The inherent conflict between Native religion and Christianity grew, as did the angry images. *The Gift* of 1975 (No. 19) epitomizes and directly confronts the anger and the white audience. It is executed in the pictographic style but all the familiar determinatives have double meanings. The white Christian befriends the Indian, extending his hand and the touch of death. The dots, used to depict power, refer here to the power of smallpox to infect and kill. The child reaches for the medicine bag of the Christian, and is infected. It is an austere and bitter work, in earth tones of browns and greens, shedding the usual allegorical approach of Indian accounts and speaking of a power the Indians could not control or understand.

By the mid-seventies Morrisseau was studying Eckankar, a holistic religion combining both Eastern and Christian spiritual concepts, and his imagery reflected the shift from conventional Christianity to a more universal concept of the soul. He began to experiment with multi-panel pieces, as in the 1977 six-part *Man Changing into Thunderbird* (No. 20). The work hails back to his earliest concerns, but the development since the 1958-60 rendering of the same theme on birch bark is astonishing. Each panel traces the transformation of human to bird form and yet the progression is not continuous. Certain human characteristics emerge and recede, until the full thunderbird identity asserts

15
Norval Morrisseau
Water Spirit 1972
Acrylic on brown mill paper
80.7 x 183.5 cm
National Museum of Man, Ottawa

itself. Any single panel could exist independently of the other, for each documents a discreet stage of change. As a whole, however, the work is a total environment that engulfs the viewer. The colour, while building on the rich stained-glass palette of the Christian icons, is now more reminiscent of traditional Indian beadwork and costume design, particularly in the multiple outlines and segmentation of the man's regalia and the thunderbird's wings.

In the 1978 two-panel image *The Story-teller: The Artist and His Grandfather* (No. 21, colour plates pp. 38-39), Morrisseau has effectively split the work to create a sense of separation. Although the two panels address each other, the grandfather, now dead, is clearly the predominant figure. His mission to salvage Ojibwa culture was passed on to his grandson, who broke with tradition to do so by becoming an artist. It is a poignant and tender image softened by the acrylic wash effect and the warmth of the reds, blues, and purples. It stands in dramatic counterpoint to the earlier Christian icons in the free flow of lines and colour, the human emotion that emanates from the figures, and the colour wash technique that enhances the sense of spontaneity. The return to Native imagery and personal themes was accompanied by a loosening or freeing up of his style. In his maturing as an artist, Morrisseau appears to be returning to or acknowledging his visual roots in Ojibwa traditions. ·

After 1978 Morrisseau, always a student of Ojibwa culture, embarked on a series of floral studies unlike the 1969 still life (No. 13), drawing instead on traditional beadwork aesthetics. In the 1979 untitled acrylic on canvas in the McMichael Collection (fig. 10), a network of living plants replaces the former stained-glass mosaic. Eschewing cut flowers, Morrisseau captures the energy of traditional design and fills the space with fantastic plant life of brilliantly contrasting colours, multiple outlines, and sensual surface texture. when compared to a beaded velvet vest made near Fort Frances in northwestern Ontario in the 1920s (fig. 11) – executed in a style Morrisseau could have seen in his youth – both share a vitality of line bristling with life, luxuriant plants, and flowers. Both employ segmented contrasting fields of colour.

The richness of the traditional decorative arts, particularly beaded costumes, can be seen in Morrisseau's aesthetic development. With the widespread introduction of European glass beads, by the nineteenth century beadwork replaced original quill and moosehair appliqué among Indian crafts. Clothing was very important and much time was devoted to its ornamentation as a source of prestige. Hides of deer, moose, caribou, bear, and elk were tanned and tailored into pouches, moccasins, leggings, breech-clouts, and vests. Techniques of embroidery, quillwork, beadwork, and ribbon appliqué were used. Soon after European contact broadcloth became available and quickly supplanted hides. According to Sister Bernard Coleman, colours of red, deep blues, and black were preferred by the Cree and Ojibwa as backgrounds for the colourful array of applied design. In the nineteenth century the Ojibwa adopted dark velveteen, usually black, despite its higher price. Black velveteen dramatically accentuated the now predominantly beaded patterns. By the late nineteenth century, Ojibwa design reached a rococo frenzy of undulating lines, bright and contrasting colours, and stylized asymmetry. Ojibwa beadwork became more linear, exhibiting preferences for multiple outlines and elaborate veining of stems and leaves. There was an increased sense of movement in the flow of these designs. Ojibwa pictography and the decorative arts shared a linear dynamism, qualities Morrisseau consciously acknowledges.

Morrisseau has come full circle in his most recent monumental scroll, *Shaman Teaching His Two Halves in a Dream State* (fig. 12), completed in 1983. In a breathtaking tribute to his roots in Ojibwa pictography, the artist has transcended his beginnings and created a surreal dream environment in which

19
Norval Morrisseau
The Gift 1975
Acrylic on kraft paper
195.7 x 122.0 cm
Collection of Helen E. Band, Toronto

A

D

20
Norval Morrisseau
Man Changing into Thunderbird 1977
Acrylic on canvas
Six panels, each 153.5 x 125.7 cm
Whetung Art Gallery, Curve Lake, Ontario

B

C

E

F

fig. 11

fig. 10

fig. 12

fig. 10 Norval Morrisseau, *Untitled (gold)*, 1979; acrylic on canvas, 120.0 x 60.0 cm. The McMichael Canadian Collection, Purchase 1979.

fig. 11 Ojibwa beaded vest c.1920 from Manitou Rapids near Fort Frances, Ontario. Royal Ontario Museum, Toronto.

fig. 12 Norval Morrisseau, central detail from *Shaman Teaching His Two Halves in a Dream State*, 1983; ink on drawing paper, 88.8 cm x 9.1 m. Collection of the artist.

the viewer inevitably loses himself. The scroll is a spiritual voyage in which the artist is both instructor and student. The scroll cannot be read or decoded for information, although the images are recognizable from the Midewiwin Society scrolls. The images do not follow left to right or up and down. They resonate with highly charged associations, like fragments of remembered dreams whose meanings are all the more evocative for being unnamable. About this scroll Morrisseau has said in a 1983 interview:

> When the Midewiwin people wrote simple bird signs – all these signs – they did that for a reason. They began to invoke that dream-state. . . . This scroll is more or less for the environment of one person . . . to feel for awhile that there is a separate reality.

Norval Morrisseau stands alone in his formal innovation and largeness of personal vision. He was the first Indian to study seriously and to update his own cultural beliefs and translate them visually for contemporary Indian and non-Indian audiences. In doing so he became the first Indian to break through the Canadian professional white-art barrier. His brilliance lies in his ability to break away from his own conventions, to constantly renew his vision.

Morrisseau eschewed a single home and travelled restlessly around Ontario and across Canada. In 1971 and 1972, he participated with other artists in two northern education tours, which spread the gospel of a new Indian art. The pictographic style of painting, as a whole inclusive visual system, was perceived in the early days as a tribal style easily adapted by other Indians. Because it was a new system, early critics and viewers found it difficult to differentiate between the artists or to evaluate their work. And yet in perspective, each artist who paints in the pictographic style must be evaluated as an artist, not as an Indian.

2   Daphne Odjig: Innovator and Pioneer

Daphne Odjig's career long preceded the development of the pictographic style of painting and in recent years has diverged from it. Odjig's contributions to the style have been in the areas of formal innovation and of transcending many traditional barriers to Indians in the arts. The pictographic style liberated her work, allowing her to express her Indianness and to deal with more personal concerns, such as identity, human values, and family life. She did not meet Morrisseau until after she encountered his work in the late sixties. She remains one of the very few Indian women artists working today.

Odjig was born in 1925 on Wikwemikong Reserve on Manitoulin Island to an Odawa father and white mother. As a child she was encouraged to draw by her father and grandfather, who both sketched. Her grandfather was a carver of tombstones. Daphne left school at fourteen due to ill health, and a few years later her mother died. After a brief stay with her grandmother, Daphne moved to Toronto. During the subsequent period of menial jobs, she continued to sketch, visit galleries, and read about European art.

In 1945 Odjig met and married Paul Sommerville and moved to Vancouver. During the ensuing years her impressionistic painting reflected a love of the British Columbia landscape, and she was elected to the B.C. Federation of Artists. In 1960 her husband was killed in an automobile crash.

In 1963 Odjig married Chester Beavon and moved to northern Manitoba, where he worked as a social development officer. It was here that she embarked on a series of pen-and-ink sketches of rural Indian life. The sketches were characterized by touching but unsentimental portraits of displacement and degeneration.

In 1967 Odjig and her husband moved to Winnipeg, and she had her first solo exhibition in Thunder Bay. She began painting legend and folklore images derivative of Northwest Coast Indian art, and experimented in collage. It was not until 1969 that she met Norval Morrisseau. From the late sixties on, her career accelerated at an ever-increasing rate, and her stylistic development in the pictographic mode coincided with growing public interest in Indian art.

In 1971 Odjig attended the Smoltra Folklore Festival in Zagreb, Yugoslavia, as part of a larger Indian delegation. She returned to Ontario and acted as an instructor at the Fine Arts Folk School for Native Students, part of the Manitou Arts Foundation on Schreiber Island. That same year she and her husband established Odjig Indian Prints and Crafts of Canada, a gallery and print distributor that became The Warehouse Gallery two years later. She completed a series of illustrated Nanabush legend books for primary schools. All of these activities facilitated her meeting with other Indian artists and established her as an educator and a pioneer; she was a "first" in many endeavours, including being the first Indian to own her own gallery and control print production.

In 1972 Odjig was included with Alex Janvier and Jackson Beardy in the Winnipeg Art Gallery's exhibition, *Treaty Numbers 23, 287, 1171: Three Indian Painters of the Prairies*. This event was the first time a public gallery had examined contemporary Indian art in Canada. In the same year the Manitoba Museum of Man and Nature commissioned her first mural, *The Creation of the World*.

The year 1973 was one of great political awareness among Native people. At about this time Professional Native Artists Inc. was formed – the "Indian Group of Seven" – consisting of Daphne Odjig, Carl Ray, Eddy Cobiness, Jackson Beardy, Alex Janvier, Joseph Sanchez, and Roy Thomas. Odjig received a scholarship to become resident artist at the Brucebo Foundation Studio in Visby, Island of Gotland, Sweden, a tribute to her work that afforded her further international travel and study.

In 1974 the book of erotic stories she illustrated for Herbert Schwarz, *Tales from the Smokehouse*, was released. In 1975 El Al Airlines commissioned her to paint her impressions of the Holy Land for a run of posters that became "The Jerusalem Series." The National Museum of Man commissioned her second major mural in 1976. The 2.4 by 8.2 metre mural, *The Indian in Transition*, was unveiled at the National Arts Centre in 1978. That year Odjig was honoured by the elders of Wikwemikong for her contributions to Indian culture. In 1982 she received an Honorary Doctorate of Letters from Laurentian University.

Of concern here is Odjig's work during her pictographic period. As far back as the early sixties, according to biographer R. Vanderburgh, Odjig was urged by friends and relatives to depict Native traditions. These relatives included Tom Pelletier, a founder of the Manitou Arts Foundation. It was not until she adapted the pictographic style that she found a form that suited this function.

An early example is *Earth Mother* of 1969 (No. 22), which was exhibited at Expo '70 in Osaka, Japan. The female figure has been abstracted and shares some pictographic conventions. At second glance, the image more clearly resembles a two-dimensional rendering of a three-dimensional concept. The face is profiled and mask-like. Details such as the headband, fringe, and zigzag decoration give a generalized impression of Indianness. The flowing curvilinear line is a dramatic departure from her naturalistic sketches of Indian life on Wikwemikong Reserve executed the year before. In this painting Odjig made a sudden transition from illustration to expressionism. The archetypal image of the earth mother recurs frequently in her work as a source of life and emotions.

Odjig did not linger long illustrating legends. Quickly she got to the heart of the stories and turned more to social issues. Her art became politicized, and its

22
Daphne Odjig
Earth Mother 1969
Acrylic on paper
91.4 x 61.0 cm
Private Collection

24
Daphne Odjig
Massacre 1971
Oil pastel on paper
62.3 x 92.5 cm
The Winnipeg Art Gallery

style became more expressively abstract. The 1971 *Massacre* (No. 24) is a powerful indictment of the slaughter at Fort Dearborn, Chicago, in 1812, in which her great-great-grandfather was involved. It is a brooding dark pastel. The rhythm of the lines expresses chaos in which human and animal forms become indistinguishable.

Odjig's social commentary can be traced to her figurative drawings of life in northern Manitoba. Moving into a more abstract mode, at first through Northwest Coast Indian art and then through the pictographic style of Morrisseau, her forms were freed to express not just outward conditions but inner significance. There is a sense of her line, like a life line, coming from her heart through her hand. The legends proved to be too stilted, too indirect to suit her purpose. Her admiration of Picasso is evident in her work, but more in the freedom of line than in any attempt to copy his style. According to Sandra Johnson, she was attracted by Picasso's "lack of inhibition" and van Gogh's "emotionalism." Her conscious interest in the European masters earned her the nickname "Madame Picasso" from Morrisseau, and led to public misinterpretations of her style as "Cubistic."

Following her mural commission from the Manitoba Museum of Man and Nature, and during the formative years of the Indian Group of Seven, Odjig encouraged her colleagues to work on a larger scale. Her own product of this period is *From Mother Earth Flows the River of Life* (No. 25, colour plate p. 42) – a vivid demonstration of how much more suited to a large scale her style really is. The central figure is the earth mother, but rendered more organic and abstract than in her 1969 interpretation. The painting incorporates the swirling textures of collage – a medium in which she has worked since 1968 – without the natural materials, using only acrylics.

The *Collage* of 1971 (No. 23, colour plate p. 40) offers an interesting comparison in its surreal exaggerated figure – particularly the enlarged cyclops' eye reminiscent of a divided ovoid. The image is rich in texture, and the pictography is abstracted to pan-Indian notations. As in *Massacre*, one is swept along by the energy of the line. Unlike *Massacre*, the image is a positive affirmation of the Indian world view or life principle. Her efforts to portray the reciprocal relationship between man and nature can be traced to her earliest landscapes of the 1940s.

Odjig selectively incorporated the linear determinatives and vocabulary of mythic forms from the pictographic style and shaped them to her own purpose. The result is a stylistic virtuosity that defies a single label. *Thunderbird Man* of 1973 (No. 26) is a powerful iconic figure that literally vibrates with energy. Odjig has employed linear determinatives of every kind: from the senses, from the fingertips, to and from the white circle of energy, and emanating from the rib cage. The life line and "heart" echo the phallus, and all energy seems to well upwards. The face is frontal and mask-like, with a profiled eagle emerging on one side like a west-coast transformation mask. The arms are in the process of becoming wings, and the legs are bird-like too. There is a sense of an alter-ego coming up from behind the human figure and engulfing or shrouding him with the thunderbird identity. The process of transformation seems to generate a vortex of energy, amplified by the ripple effect of the wavy lines. *Thunderbird Man* bears comparison to Morrisseau's images over the years of this figure – particularly the six-panel *Man Changing into Thunderbird* of 1977 (No. 20). Morrisseau's thunderbirds tend to be more emblematic. In depicting change he freezes discreet elements and serializes them. Odjig has embodied in a single image the violent merging of two identities. Both Morrisseau and Odjig excel in portraying double identities. These images that bridge two worlds are traditionally figures of great power. Represented by the artists, they afford strong

26
Daphne Odjig
Thunderbird Man 1973
Wash and oil on bristol board
72.4 x 94.0 cm
Collection of Dr. Bernhard Cinader, F.R.C.S.,
  Toronto

27
Daphne Odjig
Tribute to the Great Chiefs of the Past 1975
Acrylic on canvas
101.8 x 81.0 cm
The McMichael Canadian Collection, Purchase
  1975, 1975.11.1

28
Daphne Odjig
Conflict between Good and Evil 1975
Acrylic on canvas
81.0 x 101.2 cm
The McMichael Canadian collection, Purchase
   1975, 1975.11.3

fig. 13 Daphne Odjig, *The Indian in Transition*, 1978; acrylic on canvas, 2.4 x 8.2 m. National Museum of Man, Ottawa.

medicine for the reintegration of Indian culture suffering from social schizophrenia.

In *Tribute to the Great Chiefs of the Past* of 1975 (No. 27), Odjig presents a totemic celebration of her ancestors. The painting conveys a sculptural monumentality in its conception, with the predecessors transcending space and time. The facelessness evokes a loss of history but the energy and vibrant quality express a revitalization of Indian values. It is a foreshadowing of her later rewriting of history in *The Indian in Transition*.

Also in 1975 Odjig depicted the *Conflict between Good and Evil* (No. 28). She has created a battlefield where primeval forms vie for victory. It is a powerful statement of cultural imbalance – of life under siege as experienced by contemporary Indians, where Indian values are threatened with extinction.

The 1976-78 *The Indian in Transition* (fig. 13) is a natural development out of her previous work. Able through the National Museum of Man commission to work on the large scale she preferred, Odjig produced a work of revisionist and visionary power. The monumental painting is matched in its size by the ambition of its message. The work can be endlessly deciphered like Picasso's *Guernica*. There are fragments that are whole images in themselves. What the mural establishes, however, is that "separate reality" of which Morrisseau has spoken – a fusing of Indian experience and Indian spirituality.

The pictographic style provided Odjig with a means to express intense subjectivity and cultural identity. Her work quickly moved beyond the pictographic conventions to a more formally innovative abstract vision. Above all she has found a means to express an Indian reality, with all its tragedy and contradictions, on a scale equal to the monumental injustice and irrationality of the experience.

3 The Younger Generation

An interesting phenomenon of the pictographic style of painting is its appeal to almost three generations of Indian artists. Carl Ray is the bridge between two of these generations, between Morrisseau and the painters who reached their thirties in the early 1980s. Ray was more approachable as a person than Morrisseau and through his art was especially accessible to those younger aspiring artists. And yet he died far too young to be able to have realized his full artistic promise. His work remains frozen in time as a pristine model for others.

In dealing with the next generation of pictographic painters only four have been selected in addition to Carl Ray, but these examples do not fully convey the impact of the style as seen in Ontario today. A conservative estimate of the number of avid practitioners in or from northwestern and central Ontario would indicate that there are well over seventy-five.

CARL RAY

Carl Ray's life and work for many years parallelled those of Morrisseau. Ray depicted Cree ceremonies that continued to be practised, and Indian beliefs that continued, through legend and story-telling, to maintain a strong hold on his community. In his art he confronted his own painful struggle to heal the personal and cultural dualities that tore him apart.

Ray was born in 1943 on Sandy Lake Reserve into a family of acknowledged medicine men, his grandfather and his brother among them. He left residential school at thirteen, following the death of his father, and helped the family by hunting and trapping. Ray's earliest artistic efforts (although none are documented) met with profound suspicion and social sanction in the Native community, ostensibly for breaking Indian taboos. This period has been popularized almost to the level of myth by many authors. According to James Stevens:

> Carl Ray . . . endured the sorcery of the Sandy Lake medicine men because he dared to paint the sacred beliefs and stories. So effective was their power that Carl did not touch paint or canvas for several years.

Leaving the reserve to work in the Red Lake gold mines and acquiring, along with the job, a pattern of violent drunken behaviour, Ray developed tuberculosis and was sent to the Fort William (now Thunder Bay) sanitorium to recover. Upon returning home in 1966, he found the community attitude altered since Morrisseau's rise to prominence. Morrisseau's current residency in the community itself with his wife and children made painting a more acceptable preoccupation. Ray continued to live on the reserve as an artist, with frequent forays out. In 1978 he was killed in a drunken brawl in Sioux Lookout. He was thirty-five.

Ray's career developed in the shadow of Morrisseau's. He worked as an apprentice to Morrisseau on the mural for the Indians of Canada Pavilion of Expo '67 in Montreal. By this time Ray had developed a style of, and preference for, scenic painting. He approached the pictographic rigour of Morrisseau's work with an illustrator's interest. Ray's works from 1968 were mostly ''legends . . . painted in bright colours,'' as James Stevens has noted. He enjoyed and prided himself on being a colourist. When asked to provide black and brown ink illustrations for Stevens' book, *Sacred Legends of the Sandy Lake Cree*, Ray perceived this reversion to a more austere style as a loss of face, Stevens reported.

Yet the images from the book, released in 1971, were among the first Ray works displayed at Toronto's Aggregation Gallery in 1972. The illustrations were the southern art public's introduction to his work. The label ''legend painting'' stuck, although his work included two divergent styles reflecting northern and southern market preferences – colourful nostalgic scenes for the north, and pictographic depictions of Indian beliefs for southern buyers.

Rarely did Ray successfully combine the two styles. *Thunderbirds* of 1972-73 (No. 29, colour plate p. 43) is a powerful depiction of a traditional theme using Western conventions of perspective, foreshortening, and naturalistic detail. The sharp silhouettes are a dramatic contrast to the impressionistic application of paint in the brooding skies. Yet the pictographic linear determinatives can be seen in the eagle's extended tongue and bristled back, and in the lightning bolts, issuing from birds swooping down, that echo the shapes of the leafless trees in the lower right. The mountain crag itself possesses a tortured inner system in the labyrinth of human paths it bears.

Bang-wa-jusk of 1972 (No. 30) describes the instant at which an animal suffers punishment for disrupting the natural order by devouring a human child. The lines convey an electrifying force imposed from outside and not the

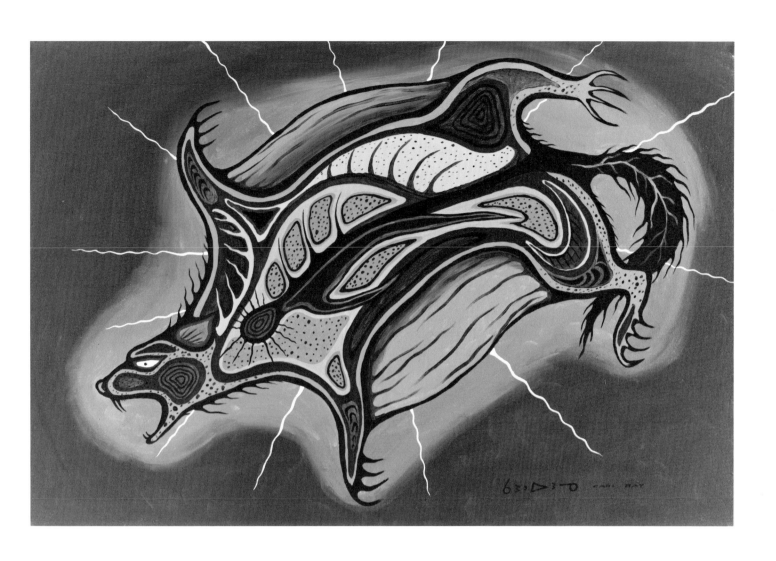

30
Carl Ray
Bang-wa-jusk, Legendary Man Eater 1972
Acrylic on canvas
72.5 x 110.0 cm
Collection of Dr. Peter K. Lewin, Toronto

wolverine's own innate spiritual power. The wolverine appears flayed like an outstretched pelt. For his transgression the wolverine and his progeny were branded with a patch of white fur, resembling an infant, on their backs – a perpetual warning to man as well. Inside the figure, the simplified outline of the child doubles as an animal skeleton, with the child's head resonating in place of the creature's heart. The wolverine's own lines of power are cursory and defunct. The browns of the animal contrast jarringly with the blues of the environment.

Ray's predilection for colour became increasingly compartmentalized in view of his southern market's preference for pictographically vivid stories that could be authenticated in the Stevens book. He had been literally typecast, and much of his work dealt with reinterpretations of the same legends.

The story-telling side of Ojibwa and Cree cultures was seized upon as an opportunity to teach Indian children their past and make them proud of their roots. In 1971 the Ontario Ministry of Education sponsored Morrisseau and Ray on a tour through Kirkland Lake, Haileybury, Timmins, Wawa, Bruce Mines, Elliot Lake, Blind River, Manitoulin Island, Sudbury, Levak, North Bay, Bracebridge, Oshawa, and Whitby. Artists of northwestern Ontario were introduced to the northeast and south in a program of affirmative action. During their visits, the artists bore witness to their art. As John Gillies explained in 1971:

> Before Carl Ray began painting for a living he tried his hand at trapping, a skill natural to him and his Native brothers. For the last month, in his own shy way, he has been telling Ontario secondary school students and community art club members that as a trapper he wasn't a success... introducing students to Ojibwa art and culture.

His article mistakenly cites Ray as an Ojibwa. The focus is on art as a job – if other ventures don't work out.

Ray was perceived as a more likeable version of Morrisseau, especially because his work was more accessible. The *Dryden Observer* reported that:

> Carl Ray's work is not primitive like the work of his contemporary, Norval Morrisseau. Instead, it has a magical realism about it; loons, bears, moose, fish, and wolves are undeniably real, but they have a supernatural quality about them.

In 1971, Ray taught at the seminal Manitou Arts Foundation on Schreiber Island, precursor of the Indian-run cultural educational centre, the Ojibwe Cultural Foundation. The following year the Department of Indian Affairs sponsored his second tour through northern communities and reserves.

At this time Ray created a full-wall-sized mural for a classroom in the Sandy Lake primary school. His only previous large-scale work had been his collaboration with Morrisseau on the Expo '67 mural for the Indians of Canada Pavilion. His own work had not increased organically in scale over the years, as had Morrisseau's, and as a result the mural is simply a blow-up of his smaller-scale style. Similarly, in the mural for the January 1971 opening of the Sioux Lookout Fellowship and Communications Centre (lost in a fire that destroyed the building soon after), the figures are larger and strung out lineally the breadth of the requisite space. The image, dedicated by the artist to his people, depicts the story of creation. In it man is only a single and unprepossessing link in a chain that includes eagle, frog, and wolf, all strung together by a serpentine line.

Ray's pictographic painting in the black, brown, and later blue formlines was embraced more readily by white buyers, who did not have to confront Morrisseau's ego or complexity. Ray presented another way of perceiving the world with enough representationalism to provide visual ''anchors'' for non-Indians.

31
Carl Ray
Medicine Bear 1973
Black ink on paper
58.7 x 73.9 cm
Collection of Dr. Bernhard Cinader, F.R.C.S.,
 Toronto

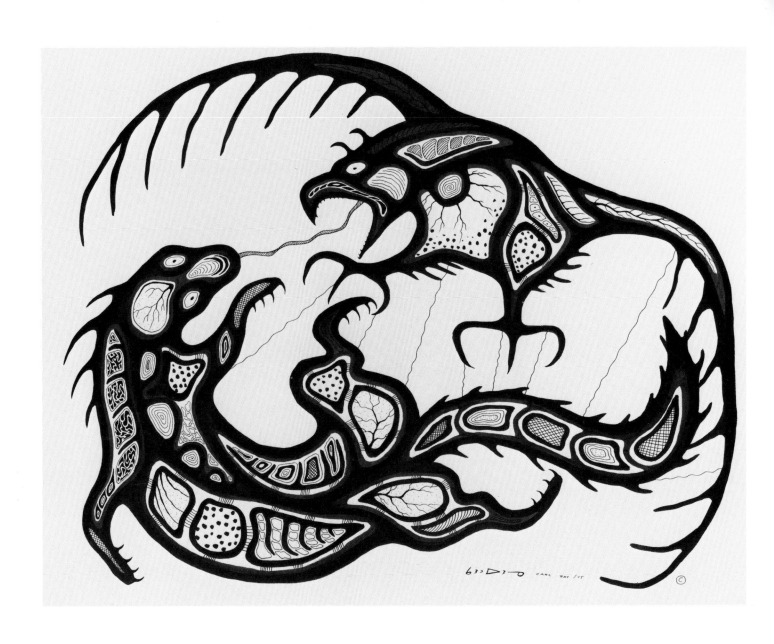

32
Carl Ray
Conflict between Good and Evil 1975
Acrylic on paper
56.0 x 75.7 cm
The McMichael Canadian Collection, Purchase
  1975, 1975.32.5

33
Carl Ray
Untitled 1975
Acrylic on paper
76.0 x 56.0 cm
The McMichael Canadian Collection, Purchase
  1975, 1975.49.3

The white viewers were attracted by the obsolescence of the culture, while Christian Indian communities were disturbed by the persistence of Indian religion. The sense of risks taken, and taboos broken, attracted everyone. However, while pictography employed for sacred functions had restricted or specialized audiences, there is no history of life-threatening taboos associated with it. It was probably Christianity and the Canadian law, which prohibited the practice of Indian religion up to 1951, that drove many beliefs and ceremonies underground. Sandy Lake, a reserve of approximately 1,200 people, was ruptured by competing Roman Catholic, United Church, Pentecostal, and Northern Light Gospel sects. The dragging out of the closet of Native beliefs must have been abhorrent to the small town. In addition, the two individuals or "role models" were volatile men who somehow reaped both white esteem and white financial remuneration for what they did. The same white society that had repressed Indian culture and outlawed Indian religion now paid to see it and sought to own a piece of it. Even more inscrutably, it was labelled distinctively Canadian art and paraded at international expositions in Montreal and Osaka.

Medicine Bear of 1973 (No. 31) epitomizes Ray's iconic pictographic mode. It is a potent double image, where the human figure within an animal produces a supernatural hybrid figure, which is neither one nor the other. The action takes place internally. The external landscape and circles are merely environmental reference points. The bear is a powerful guardian spirit in the shaking tent and the Midewiwin Society. The human may also refer to the shaman calling upon, and merging with, the spirit of the bear during the shaking tent ritual, a powerful healing ceremony performed by a shaman in a small structure or tent that has been known to move when the ceremony is at its full height. It is a strong image in its dramatic design, with the ferocious bear rushing out in one direction and the human, internal figure turned, hair streaming, mouth open, in the opposite direction. While the decorative elements – the elegant line, the segmentation and cross-hatched filler – are appealing, the linear nerve ends put one effectively off balance. The lines of various thicknesses are almost at war, and certainly serve different functions. The dual figure represents equal and opposing forces – tension and balance.

The untitled work from 1975 (No. 33) also represents Ray's work at its most literal and expository. The human torso is frontal, the self-portrait head is profiled. The creation chain is stratified like a highrise apartment. Both arms curve outwards and contain mask-like faces emanating energy. The figure is largely self-contained in spite of the four external and interconnected spheres. The wealth of specific, meticulously wrought representational detail is at odds with the non-visual or mythic reality that is portrayed, creating a compelling visual tension.

Ray added a new illustrative dimension to the iconic forms evolved by Morrisseau and in doing so created enduring images of Cree culture. These images, because of their literal qualities, conveyed the violence and delicate balance inherent in all life even more viscerally than those of his colleague. Ray lacked Morrisseau's ego and was not a shaman himself. His art, in the beginning, was less declamatory and more documentary than Morrisseau's.

By the mid-seventies Ray's work showed increasing personal references and concomitant themes of irreconcilable dualities. In 1975, the same year as Morrisseau's *The Gift* (No. 19) and Odjig's painting *Conflict between Good and Evil* (No. 28), Ray painted his own *Conflict between Good and Evil* (No. 32). It was this same period that saw the declaration of the Winnipeg-based Indian Group of Seven and the year that some of the member artists produced their most political pictures. Ray's painting confirms the fact that traditional Cree myths can be updated as powerful contemporary allegories, and can generate

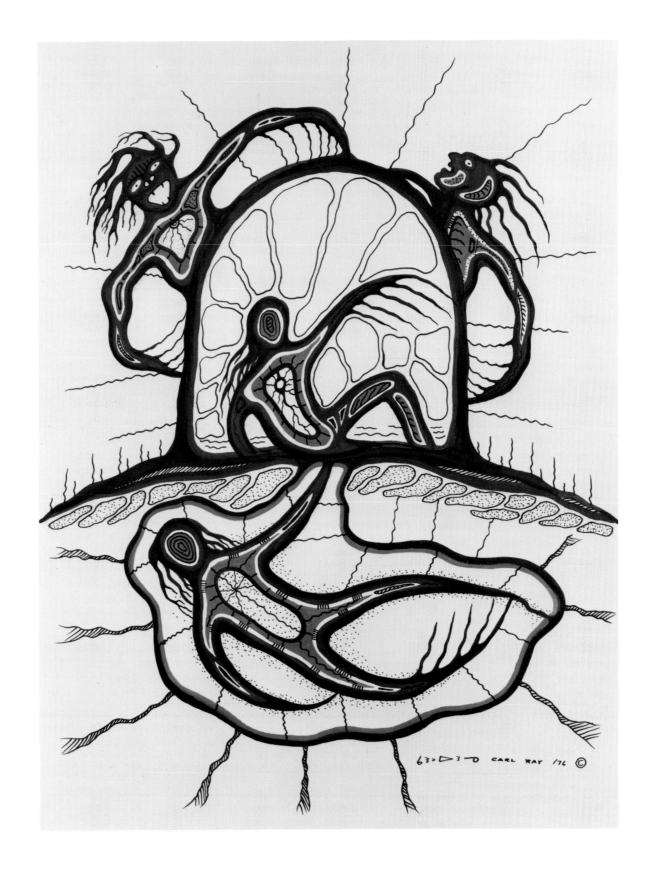

34
Carl Ray
Camping over Ancestral Grave 1976
Acrylic on paper
66.0 x 51.0 cm
Collection of Dr. Peter K. Lewin, Toronto

broad universal response. The eagle and wolverine are locked in eternal combat – good is not assured a victory. His approach is far more literal than Odjig's, embodying the two forces as identifiable figures in Cree mythology.

In the 1976 *Camping over Ancestral Grave* (No. 34), Ray takes a decidedly autobiographical turn. Having almost killed his wife in a drunken rage, he decided to stay overnight in a burial site of his predecessors, a frightening and dangerous act of atonement. The world of the living and of the dead are layered mirror images. The art itself has been used as a vehicle of exorcism. He turned to his ancestors or traditional ways for expiation from an incident very much the result of Western cultural intrusion.

The conflict and inner anguish that permeated his art remained unresolved. At the time of his death, his art had only begun to deal with Native-Christian dichotomies or realities. His preferences for colour, and his nostalgic landscapes, were not what gained him recognition. The southern white art market preferred the one- or two-colour formline images that could be explained by his book, *Sacred Legends of the Sandy Lake Cree*. It set out the parameters within which he continued to work. Like Morrisseau, Ray started painting in a more colourful, conventional Western style. Unlike Morrisseau, Ray appended the pictographic mode to his repertoire but continued to paint his preferred landscapes and genre scenes primarily for northern buyers. Ray's linear style is appealing in its lyric naturalism and spiritual expressiveness. Birds and animals are rendered in silhouettes of subtle detail, while internally the creatures are raging or changing in mysterious ways.

Ray's influence can be seen in virtually the entire second generation of northwestern Ontario and Manitoulin Island artists. His pictographic style was a training ground for many Indian youths who were offered Indian art as identity, and his value as an artist is more than the sum total of his paintings. He was a teacher.

JOSHIM KAKEGAMIC

Born in 1952 in Sandy Lake, Joshim Kakegamic enjoyed early and extensive contact with brother-in-law Norval Morrisseau and with Carl Ray. Joshim studied with Ray and Morrisseau during their tour of northern reserves. Later he joined them as a teacher himself, touring northeastern and southern schools. Following these tours, he presented a solo workshop at Fanshawe College in London, Ontario, where he first became interested in printmaking. In 1973 he, with his brothers Goyce and Henry, started the Triple K Co-operative, a silkscreen operation based in Red Lake. His first group show was in North Bay in 1969. By 1975 he was being shown at Toronto's Aggregation Gallery, which still handled Ray's work.

Kakegamic's early work expressed familiar Native images, such as the thunderbird, in confident and spider-like black formlines that enclosed a web of inner spiritual workings. Secondary earth tones were added later as filler. By the early seventies his formline grew more assertive and more emotionally expressive, often overpowering the image in its black undulations and its spiky determinatives. The scale of Kakegamic's work grew quickly and organically, as though the sheer kinetic energy could simply no longer be constrained. The serpents in *Shaking Tent* of 1973 (No. 35) are large and expressive, and bear the personal stamp of Kakegamic's overwhelming black formline. The internal segmentation is more decorative than expressive – all the more so with the flat contrasting green, gold, and ochre fillings.

Kakegamic moved easily into a classic iconic pictographic mode, mastering the forms but without possessing the substantial base of traditional knowledge that drove Morrisseau and Ray to paint. The younger artist found it difficult to

35
Josh Kakegamic
Shaking Tent 1973
Black ink on paper
72.0 x 107.8 cm
Collection of Dr. Bernhard Cinader, F.R.C.S.,
  Toronto

36
Josh Kakegamic
Three Brothers 1975
Acrylic on kraft paper
127.5 x 70.1 cm
Collection of Dr. Bernhard Cinader, F.R.C.S.,
  Toronto

37
Josh Kakegamic
Hibernation 1977-78
Acrylic on board
81.0 x 101.4 cm
Collection of John Vincett and Pamela Wheaton,
   Toronto

38
Josh Kakegamic
Awakening 1977-78
Acrylic on board
81.5 x 81.5 cm
Collection of John Vincett and Pamela Wheaton,
    Toronto

elicit information from the elders through which to exploit his style. Perhaps as a result, Kakegamic's most effective and distinctive works in his early years were those that chronicled or commemorated actual events.

In the 1975 *Three Brothers* (No. 36), Kakegamic marks the founding of Triple K. The enterprise lasted for seven years and produced fine-quality, limited-edition original prints by Indian artists in the region, including Josh and Goyce, Saul Williams, Paddy and Barry Peters, and Norval Morrisseau. The enterprise was unusual because it was an arts business located outside an urban centre, it was Native-run, and it produced a dependable product in what was fast becoming a quick-buck, unreliable Indian-print industry. In the painting, the brothers are almost canonized in their Christian icon profiles, their three respective spheres of spiritual energy. The mandala-like crescent on the upper right unifies the composition, rectifying what would otherwise be a structural imbalance.

In the 1977-78 companion pieces *Hibernation* and *Awakening* (Nos. 37, 38), Kakegamic pays tribute to and mourns the death of Carl Ray. The diptych is a powerful piece – all the more so for being allegorical in the potently compressed figure of the bear sleeping and coming back to life. Kakegamic's line is at its most controlled and restrained. It is a departure in concept for the artist and its animation technique of stop-action works by way of contrast. It has a cathartic effect and an emotional directness that eloquently express his understanding of Ray's troubled spirit and volatile talent.

Boy in the Moon of 1980 (No. 39, colour plate p. 44) features a greater sophistication in composition and colour. The title is taken from a popular story recounted by parents to their children, admonishing them to do as they are told. Here a boy, sent out to fetch a pail of snow, is dawdling by staring at the moon. In this mythical landscape, warm blue-green contrasts with the glowing areas of white-beige. The landscape has been stylized to create rich curvilinear lines and textures. Three human figures gaze at the fourth image of a young boy encased in the moon. The divided circle has become extraneous here as the human figure itself divides one of nature's spheres. Stars speckle the sky like dots of power.

Kakegamic's most recent work has evolved to a balanced synthesis of styles that is at once derivative of Morrisseau and Ray and distinctively his own. The powerful black formline has been harnessed to create a visual structure that perfectly occupies the entire canvas. No longer content to roll out huge demons the length of a given ground, Kakegamic compresses more complex imagery into a smaller space. The richness of the overall design and his distinctive, abbreviated figures all bespeak of a coming of age. Ray's preference for scenic detail was passed on to Kakegamic, along with his sense of linear design. Kakegamic's line always possessed greater boldness, and the younger artist was able to adapt more comfortably than Ray to a grander scale. Kakegamic's thick black formline at times expanded to enclose whole images in darkness. Later, the black receded and the formline became more restrained, as other colours and more complex imagery were introduced. While his predecessors invented and refined the pictographic style, Kakegamic was weaned on it, and rapidly perfected or standardized the vocabulary. He is a painter of technical virtuosity and an innovator in the field of Indian print production.

ROY THOMAS

Roy Thomas was born in 1949 near Longlac, Ontario, and was raised chiefly by his grandparents, who taught him through story-telling and encouraged him in questions about Native culture. Although he loved to draw as a child and continued drawing while in boarding school in Thunder Bay, it was not until he

41
Roy Thomas
Art of My People 1983
Acrylic on canvas
1.5 x 3.1 m
Collection of Lorraine Hullachan, Toronto

98

saw paintings by Morrisseau, Ray, and Odjig in Winnipeg that the elements of his style coalesced. He studied commercial art briefly at Confederation College in Thunder Bay.

For a number of years Thomas produced pictographic images of great charm and decorative colour. He became an able technician and drew from a wealth of stories passed on from his grandparents. Like Kakegamic, he quickly perceived image making as a career, as he has described it in 1982:

> I felt like a trapper when I first sold my paintings. A trapper stretches the animal pelts to dry, then rolls them up when dry and takes them to the H.B.C. But me, I used to paint on paper, waited for them to dry, then rolled them up and took them to galleries to sell.

Thomas' work started, and evolved, within the iconic pictographic mode. By 1981 several qualities of his style matured simultaneously to produce startlingly original works. His use of contrasting bright primary colours resembled the folk-art effect of Latin American textile cut-outs. His works expanded in scale and "breathed" more easily with the increased size. Into the imagery was injected a personal consciousness in the form of hand prints, quotations of rock paintings, and the figure of the artist.

The Eagle Will Fly of 1981 (No. 40, colour plate p. 46) is a dramatic compendium of Ojibwa pictographic images against a brilliant orange ground. The figures are united by what appears to be a continuous calligraphic line interconnecting all life forms. The source of energy, the ovoid in the centre, is bursting with traditional knowledge in the form of pictographic notations.

Art of My People of 1983 (No. 41) is a ten-foot mural-size canvas in taupe blue that continues to expand the theme and style of *The Eagle Will Fly*. But there is an added dimension of truly personal vision in the image of the artist and the attempt to integrate this new role into the continuum of Ojibwa culture. The paintbrush itself is composed of elements from animal and plant worlds; Thomas said in a 1983 interview that the paintbrush of fur and wood "is like an arrow to the artist, so he can provide himself and his family with food, clothing, and shelter." In both paintings he celebrates rock paintings and the water-washed rock faces worn away by the elements: "A little bit of the rock paintings are washed away with each wave. However, when the artist uses water to mix his paint, some of the old rock paintings come back on the paintings the artist does on canvas or paper." The large recumbent figure in *Art of My People* is the "sleeping giant" of Thunder Bay; figures in the four corners represent the four directions, the four seasons, the four stages of life.

Thomas is concerned with creating new continuities between the disparate elements of his life as an artist, by metaphorically connecting new activities to old forms. This poetic vision has been a catalyst in Thomas' work and has injected into it an immediacy and relevancy to viewers. Thomas himself prefers to use these paintings to reaffirm Indian values and world views, rather than to confront Christianity.

SAUL WILLIAMS

Saul Williams was born in 1954 at Weagamow (Round) Lake Reserve. Having painted since his youth, Williams' earliest exposure to Native imagery was in school, studying Northwest Coast Indian art, according to Dr. Mary Black. She was his earliest patron and spent two years (1969-70) as a researcher resident in his community. Williams was allowed free use of her cabin, where he soon took to painting (with the acrylics she had given him) on the brown housing paper that covered the house's insulation. He left school after grade eight to assist his father on the trapline.

His earliest teenage painting efforts were a tentative pan-Indian mix. In 1971 he attended a summer art program at Elliot Lake, and in 1972 the Manitou Arts Foundation on Schreiber Island. Weagamow Lake was on the Morrisseau-Ray art tour itinerary and Williams was influenced by the two artists.

By this time he had adopted a pictographic style and a cast of Ojibwa characters. The animated effect was amplified by an abundant use of all types of linear determinatives. At first, colour was limited to filler. From the beginning Williams demonstrated a lyrical line and draughtsmanship, which he exercised through portraits and life studies in pen-and-ink sketches.

By 1973 Williams' iconography and palette had become richer and more complex. *Medicine Man's Dream of Christ* of 1973 (No. 42, colour plate p. 45) features a dream, recounted to him by a friend, of Christ smoking a ten-stemmed pipe. It is a rare frontal image. Christ's body is composed of an upright fish, evoking one of the oldest Christian images, Christ the fish. The fish also looms large in Ojibwa cosmology as a major source of food, and so a force upon which Indians depend. Christ wears a crown of thistles and thorns and is smoking a pipe in the ancient ceremonial peace-making gesture. From the ten pipe bowls and the figure's open mouth rise white streams of smoke. These wavy lines of smoke, the black lines from the feathers and garland of thistles, and the curved outline of the fish serve descriptive and symbolic purposes. The dots in the fish and in the pipe bowls enhance the linear determinatives also echoed by the circles repeated in the fish/human eyes, the feathers and the thistles. The strange green helmet becomes a halo, amplified by the resonating white light or aura, which emanates from the figure. The image is a seamless synthesis of Native-Christian iconography.

The ten-stemmed pipe functions as a skeletal structure of both fish and figure. The fish becomes a stylized decorative robe. The colours are liturgical deep blues and purples. Williams has created, for contemplation, an image full of spiritual resonance.

In *Berry Picking* of 1975 (No. 43) the artist derives an image of ritual communion from a banal activity. The three figures share an apostolic gaze and have paused to acknowledge the source of the food. The berries, speckled with white dots, are received like manna from heaven. The interconnectedness or reciprocity of life is conveyed by more than linear determinatives. Williams' human faces are more naturalistically rendered, with the figures arrayed in richly coloured garments that bear emblems or attributes. The artist has created his own ancestor figures close in spirit to those of Morrisseau.

In the 1979-80 *Homage to Morrisseau* (No. 44), the older artist is transformed into an ancestor figure himself. The pose is derivative of Morrisseau's ancestor figures, as is the headdress and ceremonial robe. The serpents of sexual temptation continue to haunt Morrisseau here as they do in his self-portraits, although they have lost their stranglehold. The entire image is reminiscent of the funerary images of the Egyptian ruler, King Tut. The *Treasures of Tutankhamun* exhibition was at the Art Gallery of Ontario during the period the artist was creating this image in Toronto. The entire image can be decoded to discover the personal significance of each element to the artist, as Beth Southcott did in her interview with him in 1982:

> The white space behind Morrisseau... "represents the white man's world which he penetrated and from which he won respect."... Saul said that the drum, rattles and medicine bag held by Morrisseau are symbolic of shamanistic power and are held up against his chest to signify that he paints from the heart. The halo... is used here to signify "a gift that he has mastered and shared."

43
Saul Williams
Berry Picking 1975
Acrylic on paper
56.2 x 76.4 cm
Collection of John Vincett and Pamela Wheaton,
   Toronto

44
Saul Williams
Homage to Morrisseau 1979-80
Acrylic on canvas board
59.0 x 50.0 cm
Private Collection

45
Saul Williams
White Women and Their Plants c. 1978
Acrylic on paper
76.5 x 56.6 cm
Royal Ontario Museum, Toronto

Saul drew a diagram and indicated that the designs over the cranial area signify knowledge. The dramatic treatment of the white about the eye "was one of my experiments, the white represents emotion, tears, frustration and foresight." At the base of the throat Morrisseau wears a bird symbolic of his guardian spirits. . . . In the immediate foreground is found a recurring motif of Saul Williams, the stylized location for the subject . . . Weagamow Lake. . . . Incorporated in the blue band symbolic of protection is a golden disc which Saul states is "the Sun, plus manitou symbol, an all-in-one package!"

When I asked Saul if the symbols used . . . would apply in another painting . . . he replied "No."

Like scroll pictography, pictographic painting can only be fully deciphered by the artist. The power of the painting lies in its ability to generate viewer response quite apart from its informational value. Meaning is created while a viewer interacts with the work. Breaking the artist's code can constrict the visual possibilities, and can restrict the perception of it as art.

Williams creates rich surfaces, using white as positive colour and not just background. The entire picture plane is utilized, broken up and filled with warm colours, ornate linear notations, and symbolic flourishes. In *White Women and Their Plants* from about 1978 (No. 45), Williams has created an enigmatic image of women's white faces blossoming forth from the exuberant plant life that overflows the pots. He casts an amused eye at the inexplicable obsession of whites with bringing plants inside the home for no useful purpose, a habit he notes is increasingly being adopted by Indian women. At the same time that Morrisseau was executing painted floral designs derivative of Ojibwa beadwork, Williams was creating an image of jewel-like colours and flamboyant formlines. There is a dream-like intensity that invites the viewer simply to get lost in it.

Saul Williams' work falls within the iconic pictographic phase and appears to be moving towards an eventual confrontation of Native and Christian dichotomies. Already his imagery incorporates and comments upon white values and society. His iconography is intensely personal and excels at expressing spiritual values embodied in human figures, rather than in mythic birds or animals. His art at its best deals with art making, with being an artist – like the *Homage to Morrisseau*, Thomas' *Art of My People*, and Kakegamic's *Three Brothers* and his tribute to Ray, *Hibernation* and *Awakening*. As with all pictographic painting, Williams' art needs to be experienced intuitively, rather than interpreted or scanned for information.

BLAKE DEBASSIGE

Blake Debassige was born in 1956 in West Bay, Manitoulin Island. He studied art briefly at Elliot Lake, and Native Studies at Laurentian University in Sudbury. But more influential was his meeting with Carl Ray. Debassige attended the Manitou Arts Foundation summer program on Schreiber Island in 1972, and his first one-man show was held the next year at the Ontario Institute for Studies in Education in Toronto. Later he produced paintings for poster designs for the Ojibwe Cultural Foundation in West Bay.

Debassige is one of many second-generation artists on Manitoulin Island influenced by Ray, and by the stimulus of Indian-run art programs. With the establishment of the Ojibwe Cultural Foundation in 1973-74, a whole process of conscious retrieval and encouragement of Indian culture ensued on the island. Of first importance was the elders' program, which sought to engage local elderly residents in setting out wisdom and knowledge for the young to carry on. This nurturing atmosphere encouraged an interchange between young

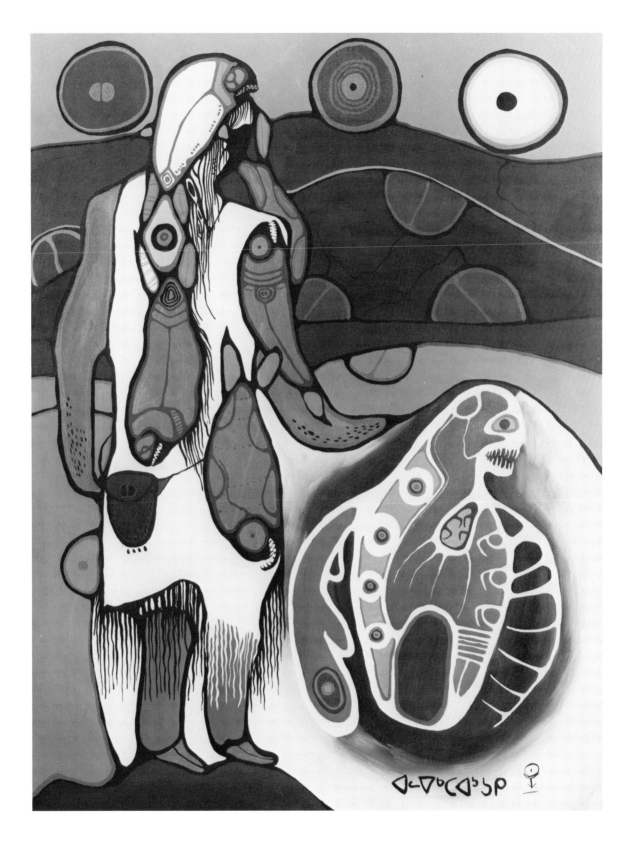

46
Blake Debassige
Woman in White Buckskin 1975-76
Acrylic on canvas
101.6 x 137.2 cm
Collection of Dr. Bernhard Cinader, F.R.C.S.,
   Toronto

49
Blake Debassige
Lonely Vigil 1982
Acrylic on canvas
132.1 x 121.9 cm
Woodland Indian Cultural Educational Centre,
  Brantford

artists and elders that continues today. Artists were drawn in as teachers.

In 1982, Debassige and his wife, painter Shirley Cheechoo, opened their own gallery on the reserve. Of the many young artists from Manitoulin Island, Debassige has been painting the longest and his work reflects the most mature growth.

In the 1975-76 *Woman in White Buckskin* (No. 46), Blake's work has evolved from the early legends, done in black and brown formline on white background, to a more personalized style that addresses contemporary issues. The title refers to a dream, documented by Bernhard Cinader in *Contemporary Indian Art*, that the artist had following the suicides of several teenagers in the neighbouring reserve of Wikwemikong. In the dream, a young girl appeared, draped with fish, with a message concerning the death – a message no one could understand. It was a troubled image from a depressing period. The image is a haunting commentary through which the dead hang like spectres over the future unless change occurs.

In *One Who Lives under the Water* of 1978 (No. 47, colour plate p. 48), Debassige acknowledges his pictographic roots in a technically sophisticated rendering of the Agawa underwater-panther rock painting. Compared to Morrisseau's 1974 depiction of the same figure, *Water Spirit* (No. 15), Debassige's style is highly decorative, displaying more awareness of the whole picture, and has a line that is more controlled and less emotional. In the dark shapeless landscape, the figure looms like a dream image.

Debassige has mastered this iconic phase of the style and has moved on to incorporate ritualized images of daily life, influenced no doubt by the genre painting of his wife. More than any other young artist Debassige has sought out and risen to the challenge of mural commissions. As with his older colleagues, Debassige's work has blossomed on a larger scale. The restrictions of the commissions have been transformed into brilliant innovations.

In *Tree of Life* (No. 48, colour plate p. 47) Debassige has created a mystical image of Christ on the cross or tree of life. His appreciation of Ojibwa design is no more self-evident than in the decorative structure of the branches, leaves, and whimsical birds/apostles. The whole effect is of a congenial fusion of Native and Christian beliefs and images into an almost animistic icon of his personal vision.

In the 1982 *Lonely Vigil* (No. 49) Debassige's vision has become an austere image of contemporary anomie, embodied in the figure of the spirit quester seeking oneness and enlightenment. The image speaks of the role of the artist, of the displacement of Indian values, and of the mission of the artist to reinstate them. It is a disturbing image and an important departure in subject and style, away from the traditional themes of story-telling towards a personal chronicle of the artist's own life.

The northern art tours by Morrisseau and Ray and the Schreiber Island summer art programs cannot be overestimated in their value as catalysts for contemporary Indian painting. An entire second generation of Indian youth was offered "Indian art" as a key to identity, white esteem, and economic self-sufficiency. This second generation mastered the techniques but frequently lacked the motivation or substance that effective painting demands. They were taught to paint like Indians, as if it were a racial predisposition. The pictographic style invented by Morrisseau was offered as an Indian mantle one could assume, as though one size would fit all. Indian communities received very little other arts input that could balance the picture of the nature of an artist. The sheer number of followers now on the art market testifies to this phenomenon.

Two regional Ontario styles can be perceived within this pictographic mode. Northwestern Ontario artists (Morrisseau, Ray, Kakegamic, Williams, and Thomas) prefer the expressive black formline that segments and interconnects all colours and figures. The subject matter tends to third-person oral traditions. The artists work in relative isolation from each other. On Manitoulin (Odjig's and Debassige's work) there is a preference for spidery lines, blended colours, and sophisticated textures. The subjects stress human values. The artists share a sense of geographical community under the nurturing auspices of the Ojibwe Cultural Foundation.

Morrisseau's pictographic style was picked up at the fully developed iconic phase by other artists. This phase is characterized by classic rendering of legendary and allegorical images. Into this was eventually injected the white presence, a blending of Native and Christian images, which culminated in the work of a few artists in a crisis of Native and Christian dichotomies. Some, like Odjig, resolved these and moved to a renewed personal vision that incorporates or synthesizes native values and contemporary experience.

The pictographic style is one that begins as culturally specific or exclusive, a discipline that demands increasing knowledge of the culture and one's self. Paradoxically it leads, as in Morrisseau's and Odjig's work, to a super-reality that is universal in its spiritual truths.

The achievement of having invented and refined the style belongs to Morrisseau. The emerging younger artists are the beneficiaries of the legacy and have painted exclusively in this style. The true talent of the second generation will be tested in their ability to find freedom within or without the pictographic conventions and to personalize both the forms and function of the art. For while Morrisseau and Odjig have paved the way as mature artists for their younger colleagues, these younger artists barely in their thirties are really only beginning. The work created in recent years is a mere glimpse of the images to come. Whatever the future directions of this style, the Indian image maker has found a permanent place in both Indian and white worlds.

Artists' Biographies

Blake Debassige

Born: 1956 West Bay Reserve, Manitoulin Island, Ontario
Art Media: Acrylic on canvas, paper
Art Education: Self-taught

GROUP EXHIBITIONS

1973   Chingaucousy Library Gallery, Bramalea, Ontario
1974   *Canadian Indian Art '74*, Royal Ontario Museum, Toronto
1974   *Contemporary Native Arts of Ontario*, Oakville Centennial Gallery, Ontario
1975   *Woodland Indian Art*, McMichael Canadian Collection, Kleinburg, Ontario
1976   *Contemporary Native Art of Canada – The Woodland Indians*, Royal Ontario Museum, Toronto, for travel to Canada House Art Gallery, London, England, and Aula Luisen Schule, Lahr, West Germany
1976   Walter Engel Gallery, Toronto, Ontario
1977   *Indian Artists and their Art*, Ojibwe Cultural Foundation, West Bay, Ontario
1977   *Contemporary Indian Art – The Trail from the Past to the Future*, Mackenzie Gallery and Native Studies Programme, Trent University, Peterborough, Ontario
1978   *Art of the Woodland Indian*, McMichael Canadian Collection, Kleinburg, Ontario
1978   *Contemporary Native Art of Canada – Manitoulin Island*, Royal Ontario Museum, Toronto
1979   *Kinder des Nanabush*, from the McMichael Canadian Collection, Kleinburg, Ontario, for Hamburg, West Germany
1979   Gallery of American Indians, New York City, N.Y.
1980   *Anishnawbe Mee-Kun*, Ojibwe Cultural Foundation, West Bay, Ontario
1981   *Native Art Auction*, Native Canadian Centre, Toronto, Ontario
1981   *Art Amerindian '81*, National Arts Centre, Ottawa, Ontario
1982   *Second National Native Art Auction*, Native Canadian Centre, Toronto, Ontario
1983   *Indian Art '83*, Woodland Indian Cultural Educational Centre, Brantford, Ontario
1983   *Last Camp, First Song: Indian Art from the Royal Ontario Museum*, organized by the Thunder Bay National Exhibition Centre, Ontario

SOLO EXHIBITIONS

1973   Ontario Institute for Studies in Education, Toronto
1973   Samual Zacks Gallery, York University, Toronto, Ontario
1974   Gallery 103, Toronto, Ontario
1974   Walter Engel Gallery, Toronto, Ontario
1976   Laurentian University Museum and Arts Centre, Sudbury, Ontario
1977   Walter Engel Gallery, Toronto, Ontario
1978   Whetung Art Gallery, Curve Lake, Ontario
1978   The Art Gallery of Peterborough, Ontario
1978   Tundra Gallery, Sault Ste. Marie, Ontario
1979   Rothmans Gallery, Sudbury, Ontario
1980   Gallery Manfred, Dundas, Ontario
1981   Nancy Poole's Studio, Toronto, Ontario
1982   Nancy Poole's Studio, Toronto, Ontario

COLLECTIONS

CIL Corporate Collection, Toronto, Ontario
Department of Indian Affairs and Northern Development, Ottawa, Ontario
Enook Galleries, Waterloo, Ontario
Glenhyrst Arts Council, Brantford, Ontario
Hospital for Sick Children, Toronto, Ontario
London Regional Art Gallery, Ontario
McMichael Canadian Collection, Kleinburg, Ontario
National Museum of Man, Ottawa, Ontario
New College, University of Toronto, Ontario
Ojibwe Cultural Foundation, West Bay, Ontario
Petro-Canada, Calgary, Alberta
Royal Ontario Museum, Toronto

COMMISSIONS

Anishnabe Spiritual Centre, Espanola, Ontario (mural)
Chingaucousy Centennial Park, Bramalea, Ontario
Ojibwe Cultural Foundation, West Bay, Ontario (6 posters)
Ontario Police Academy, Aylmer, Ontario
Mississauga Roman Catholic Church, Mississauga, Ontario (mural)
West Bay Sport Centre, West Bay, Ontario (3 murals)

Joshim Kakegamic

Born: 1952 Sandy Lake Reserve, Ontario
Art Media: Acrylic on canvas, silkscreen prints
Art Education: Self-taught

SELECTED EXHIBITIONS

1974   *Contemporary Native Arts of Ontario*, Oakville Centennial Gallery, Ontario
1975   *Indian Art '75*, Woodland Indian Cultural Educational Centre, Brantford, Ontario
1975   Aggregation Gallery, Toronto, Ontario
1976   Shayne Gallery, Montreal, Quebec
1976   *Contemporary Native Art of Canada – The Woodland Indians*, Royal Ontario Museum, Toronto, for travel to Canada House Art Gallery, London, England, and Aula Luisen Schule, Lahr, West Germany
1977   *Contemporary Indian Art – The Trail from the Past to the Future*, Mackenzie Gallery and Native Studies Programme, Trent University, Peterborough, Ontario
1977   Aggregation Gallery, Toronto, Ontario
1977   Alice Peck Gallery, Burlington, Ontario
1977   *Contemporary Native Art of Canada – Triple K Co-operative*, Royal Ontario Museum, Toronto
1978   *Art of the Woodland Indian*, McMichael Canadian Collection, Kleinburg, Ontario
1978   Aggregation Gallery, Toronto, Ontario
1978   *Indian Art '78*, Woodland Indian Cultural Educational Centre, Brantford, Ontario
1979   Aggregation Gallery, Toronto, Ontario
1980   New College, University of Toronto, Ontario
1981   *Indian Art '81*, Woodland Indian Cultural Educational Centre, Brantford, Ontario
1981   *Native Art Auction*, Native Canadian Centre, Toronto, Ontario
1982   *Second National Native Art Auction*, Native Canadian Centre, Toronto, Ontario
1983   *Last Camp, First Song: Indian Art from the Royal Ontario Museum*, organized by the Thunder Bay National Exhibition Centre, Ontario

COLLECTIONS

Hospital for Sick Children, Toronto, Ontario
McMichael Canadian Collection, Kleinburg, Ontario
National Museum of Man, Ottawa, Ontario
New College, University of Toronto, Ontario
Peat, Marwick, Mitchell and Co. Ltd., Toronto, Ontario
Royal Ontario Museum, Toronto
Simon Fraser University Art Centre, Burnaby, B.C.
Woodland Indian Cultural Educational Centre, Brantford, Ontario

COMMISSIONS

Painting of Katri Tekakwitha for Sunday Mass Book, Canadian Catholic Conference, Ottawa, Ontario

Norval Morrisseau

Born: March 14, 1932
       Sand Point Reserve, near Beardmore, Ontario
Art Media: Drawing, acrylic painting, silkscreen
Art Education: Self-taught

GROUP EXHIBITIONS

1963   Kitchener-Waterloo Art Gallery, Kitchener, Ontario
1963   *Canadian Contemporary Art*, Canadian National Exhibition, Toronto, Ontario.
1965   University of Waterloo Art Gallery, Ontario
1967   Expo '67, Montreal, Quebec
1971   *Festival of Canada*, Roberson Art Centre, Binghampton, New York
1973   *Canadian Contemporary Painting*, University of Waterloo Art Gallery, Ontario
1973   *Canadian Indian Painting*, Royal Ontario Museum, Toronto
1974   McMichael Canadian Collection, Kleinburg, Ontario
1974   *Canadian Indian Art '74*, Royal Ontario Museum, Toronto
1974   *Contemporary Native Arts of Ontario*, Oakville Centennial Gallery, Oakville, Ontario
1975   Dominion Gallery, Montreal, Quebec
1975   Wallack Gallery, Ottawa, Ontario
1976   Bergens Kunsfoeing, Bergen, Norway
1976   *Contemporary Native Art of Canada – The Woodland Indians*, Royal Ontario Museum, Toronto, for travel to Canada House Art Gallery, London, England, and Aula Luisen Schule, Lahr, West Germany
1977   *Painting Now*, Agnes Etherington Art Centre, Queen's University, Kingston, Ontario
1977   *Contemporary Indian Art – The Trail from the Past to the Future*, Mackenzie Gallery and Native Studies Programme, Trent University, Peterborough, Ontario
1977   *Modern Native Canadian Art,* Hart House Gallery, University of Toronto, Ontario
1977   *Art to Go*, Art Gallery of Ontario, Toronto
1977   *McMichael Canadian Collection*, Algoma Fall Festival, Sault Ste. Marie, Ontario
1977   Government of Ontario Art Collection, Toronto
1977   *Links to a Tradition*, Department of Indian Affairs and Northern Development, for travel to centres in Brazil
1978   *Morrisseau/Thomas/Odjig*, Pollock Gallery, Toronto, Ontario
1978   *Art of the Woodland Indian*, McMichael Canadian Collection, Kleinburg, Ontario; travelled to Surrey, B. C., St. Thomas, Ontario, and North Bay, Ontario
1978   *Images of Man in Canadian Painting 1878-1978*, McIntosh Gallery, University of Western Ontario, London
1978   Glenbow-Alberta Institute, Calgary, Alberta
1978   Vancouver Art Gallery, B.C.
1978   Art Gallery of Ontario, Toronto
1978   Beaverbrook Art Gallery, Fredericton, N.B.
1979   Thunder Bay National Exhibition Centre, Ontario
1979   Timmins Museum & National Exhibition Centre, Ontario
1979   *Kinder des Nanabush*, McMichael Canadian Collection, for Hamburg, West Germany
1982   *Masterworks of Contemporary Indian Art from the National Museum of Man*, organized by the Thunder Bay National Exhibition Centre, Thunder Bay, Ontario

1983   *Contemporary Indian Art at Rideau Hall*, Department of Indian Affairs and Northern Development, Ottawa, Ontario

SOLO EXHIBITIONS

1962   Pollock Gallery, Toronto, Ontario
1963   Pollock Gallery, Toronto, Ontario
1965   Hart House Gallery, University of Toronto, Ontario
1966   St. Paul de Vence, France
1967   Musée du Québec, Quebec City
1972   Pollock Gallery, Toronto, Ontario
1974   Bau-Xi Gallery, Toronto, Ontario
1974   Pollock Gallery, Toronto, Ontario
1975   Shayne Gallery, Montreal, Quebec
1975   Pollock Gallery, Toronto, Ontario
1976   Gallery 115, Winnipeg, Manitoba
1976   Pollock Gallery, Toronto, Ontario
1977   Graphic Gallery, Vancouver, B.C.
1977   Pollock Gallery, Toronto, Ontario
1978   First Canadian Place, Toronto, Ontario
1979   Pollock Gallery, Toronto, Ontario
1979   The Gallery/Stratford, Stratford, Ontario
1979   Cardigan-Milne Gallery, Winnipeg, Manitoba
1981   Anthony's Gallery, Toronto and Vancouver
1981   Thunder Bay National Exhibition Centre, Ontario
1982   Moore Gallery Ltd., Hamilton, Ontario
1982   Masters Gallery, Calgary, Alberta
1982   Robertson Gallery, Ottawa, Ontario
1982   Scarborough Public Library, Ontario
1982   Legacy Art Gallery, Toronto, Ontario
1983   Art Imperial Gallery, Toronto, Ontario
1983   Thunder Bay National Exhibition Centre, Ontario
1983   Native American Center for the Living Arts, Niagara Falls, N.Y.

COLLECTIONS

Art Gallery of Ontario, Toronto
Art Gallery of Windsor, Ontario
Canada Council Art Bank, Ottawa, Ontario
Candian Imperial Bank of Commerce, Toronto, Ontario
Citicorp of Canada Ltd., Toronto, Ontario
City of Toronto, Ontario
Constellation Hotel, Toronto, Ontario
Crown Life Insurance, Toronto, Ontario
Davies Ward and Beck, Toronto, Ontario
Department of Indian Affairs and Northern Development, Ottawa, Ontario
Dodds Coal Mines, Edmonton, Alberta
Etobicoke Board of Education, Ontario
Glenbow Museum, Calgary, Alberta
Gordon Jones Programming Ltd., Toronto, Ontario
Guardian Capital Group, Toronto, Ontario
Hart House Art Gallery, University of Toronto, Ontario
Humber College, Toronto, Ontario
Manufacturers' Hanover Leasing Ltd., Toronto, Ontario
McMichael Canadian Collection, Kleinburg, Ontario
Montreal Museum of Fine Arts, Quebec
Musée du Québec, Quebec City
National Museum of Man, Ottawa, Ontario
Noranda Mines, Toronto, Ontario

Norcen Energy Resources
Ontario Centennial Committee Collection, Toronto
Osler, Harcourt and Hoskin, Toronto, Ontario
Proctor and Gamble, Toronto, Ontario
Roberson Art Center, Binghampton, N.Y.
Ross Memorial Hospital, Lindsay, Ontario
Royal Ontario Museum, Toronto
Sayers and Associates, Toronto, Ontario
Seneca College, Toronto, Ontario
Toronto Star Newspaper, Ontario

PUBLICATIONS

Dewdney, Selwyn, ed. *Legends of My People, The Great Ojibway*. Toronto: Ryerson Press, 1965.
Pollock, Jack and Lister Sinclair. *The Art of Norval Morrisseau*. Toronto: Methuen Publications, 1979.
Schwarz, Herbert T. *Windigo and Other Tales of the Ojibways*. Toronto: McClelland and Stewart, 1969.

COMMISSIONS

Indians of Canada Pavilion, Expo '67, Montreal, Quebec
McMichael Canadian Collection, Kleinburg, Ontario

PUBLIC GIFT

1983   *The Shaman's Androgyny*, mural 4 × 6.5 m presented by the artist to the people of Canada. On view at the Indian Affairs Building in Hull, Quebec.

AWARDS

1970   Royal Canadian Academy of Art
1978   Order of Canada

FILMS

1974   *The Paradox of Norval Morrisseau*, National Film Board of Canada
1974   *Colours of Pride*, National Film Board of Canada
1982   *Spirits Speaking Through: Canadian Woodland Artists*, CBC Spectrum Series

Daphne Odjig

Born: 1925 Wikwemikong Reserve, Manitoulin Island, Ontario
Art Media: Acrylic, pastel, collage, silkscreen prints
Art Education: Self-taught
Related Employment: 1971 – Instructor at Manitou Arts Foundation, Schreiber Island, Ontario; 1971-76 – Owner of Wah-sa Gallery, Winnipeg, Manitoba

GROUP EXHIBITIONS

1970	Minot State University, North Dakota
1970	Canadian Guild of Crafts, Montreal, Quebec
1970	Canadian Pavilion, Expo '70, Osaka, Japan
1971	L'Agence de Co-operation Culturelle et Technique, Canada, France, Belgium
1972	*Treaty Numbers 23, 287, 1171: Three Indian Painters of the Prairies*, Winnipeg Art Gallery, Manitoba
1973	Gallery Anthropos, London, England
1974	Janet Ian Cameron Gallery, University of Manitoba, Winnipeg
1974	Oakville Centennial Gallery, Ontario
1975	Winnipeg Art Gallery, Manitoba
1975	*Native Arts Festival*, Niagara-on-the-Lake, Ontario
1975	Dominion Gallery, Montreal, Quebec
1975	Wallack Gallery, Ottawa, Ontario
1975	Art Emporium, Vancouver, B.C.
1975	*Indian Art '75*, Woodland Indian Cultural Educational Centre, Brantford, Ontario
1976	*From Women's Eyes: Women Painters in Canada*, Agnes Etherington Art Centre, Queen's University, Kingston, Ontario
1976	Etobicoke Civic Centre, Ontario
1976	Janet Ian Cameron Gallery, University of Manitoba, Winnipeg
1976	*Indian Art '76*, Woodland Indian Cultural Educational Centre, Brantford, Ontario
1976	*Contemporary Native Art of Canada—The Woodland Indians*, Royal Ontario Museum, Toronto, for travel to Canada House Art Gallery, London, England, and Aula Luisen Schule, Lahr, West Germany
1977	*Links to a Tradition*, Department of Indian Affairs and Northern Development, for travel to centres in Brazil
1977	*Modern Native Canadian Art*, Hart House Art Gallery, University of Toronto, Ontario
1977	Kinsmen Centre, Calgary, Alberta
1978	*One Hundred Years of Native American Painting*, Oklahoma City Museum of Art, Oklahoma City
1982	*Renewal – Masterworks of Contemporary Indian Art from the National Museum of Man*, organized by the Thunder Bay National Exhibition Centre for Indian Art, Thunder Bay, Ontario
1983	*Contemporary Indian Art at Rideau Hall*, Department of Indian Affairs and Northern Development, Ottawa, Ontario

SOLO EXHIBITIONS

1967	Lakehead Art Centre, Port Arthur, Ontario
1968	Brandon University, Brandon, Manitoba
1969	Viscount Corte Motor Hotel, Winnipeg, Manitoba
1970	International Peace Gardens
1971	Smoltra Folklore Festival, Zagreb, Yugoslavia
1974	Warehouse Gallery of Native Art, Winnipeg, Manitoba
1976	Bashford and Schwarz Gallery, Calgary, Alberta
1977	Wah-sa Gallery, Winnipeg, Manitoba
1977	Images for a Canadian Heritage, Vancouver, B.C.
1977	Lefebre Gallery, Edmonton, Alberta
1979	Pollock Gallery, Toronto, Ontario
1979	Griffin Galleries, West Vancouver, B.C.
1980	Children of the Raven Gallery, Vancouver, B.C.
1980	Assiniboia Gallery, Regina, Saskatchewan
1981	Children of the Raven Gallery, Vancouver, B.C.
1982	Assiniboia Gallery, Regina, Saskatchewan
1983	Shayne Gallery, Montreal, Quebec

COLLECTIONS

Art Bank, Canada Council, Ottawa, Ontario
Brandon University, Manitoba
Department of Indian Affairs and Northern Development, Ottawa
Government of Israel, Jerusalem
Manitoba Government Legislature, Winnipeg
Manitoba Indian Brotherhood, Winnipeg
McMichael Canadian Collection, Kleinburg, Ontario
Museum of Man and Nature, Winnipeg, Manitoba
National Museum of Man, Ottawa, Ontario
Peguis High School, Hodgson, Manitoba
Sir Wilfrid Laurier University, Kitchener, Ontario
Tom Thomson Memorial Gallery, Owen Sound, Ontario
Winnipeg Art Gallery, Manitoba

COMMISSIONS

Centennial Commission from the Manitoba Museum of Man and Nature, Winnipeg, *The Creation of the World* (mural)
El Al Airlines, "The Jerusalem Series"
National Museum of Man, Ottawa, Ontario, *The Indian in Transition* (mural)

AWARDS

1971	Arts Grants for tour and exhibition of painting at the Smoltra Folklore Festival, Zagreb, Yugoslavia
1973	Brucebo Foundation Scholarship, and position as resident artist at the Foundation Studio in Visby, Island of Gotland, Sweden
1973	Manitoba Arts Council Bursary
1977	Canada Silver Jubilee Medal
1982	Honorary Doctorate of Letters, Laurentian University, Sudbury, Ontario

PUBLICATIONS

Odjig, Daphne. *Tales of Nanabush*. Toronto: Ginn and Co., 1971.
Schwarz, Herbert. *Tales from the Smokehouse*. Edmonton: Hurtig Publishers, 1974.

Carl Ray

Born: 1943 Sandy Lake Reserve, Ontario; died 1978

Art Education: Self-taught

Related Employment: 1971 – Instructor at Manitou Arts Foundation;
1971-1972 – Northern Art Tour sponsored by the Government of
Ontario and DIAND; Editor of *Kitiwin*, the Sandy Lake newspaper

GROUP EXHIBITIONS

1974 *Canadian Indian Art '74*, Royal Ontario Museum, Toronto

1974 *Contemporary Native Arts of Ontario*, Oakville Centennial Gallery,
Ontario

1976 *Contemporary Native Art of Canada – The Woodland Indians*,
Royal Ontario Museum, Toronto, for travel to Canada House Art
Gallery, London, England, and Aula Luisen Schule, Lahr, West
Germany

1977 *Contemporary Indian Art – The Trail From the Past to the Future*,
Mackenzie Gallery and Native Studies Programme, Trent University,
Peterborough, Ontario

1978 *Art of the Woodland Indian*, McMichael Canadian Collection, Kleinburg, Ontario

1979 *Kinder des Nanabush*, from the McMichael Canadian Collection,
Kleinburg, Ontario, for Hamburg, West Germany

1980 *Contemporary Woodland Indian Painting*, New College, University
of Toronto, Ontario

1983 *Contemporary Indian Art at Rideau Hall*, Department of Indian
Affairs and Northern Development, Ottawa, Ontario

SOLO EXHIBITIONS

1969 Brandon University, Manitoba

1970 Confederation College, Thunder Bay, Ontario

1971 Fort Frances Public Library, Ontario

1972 University of Minnesota, Minneapolis

1972 Gallerie Fore, Winnipeg, Manitoba

1972-

1977 Aggregation Gallery, Toronto, Ontario

COMMISSIONS

Indians of Canada Pavilion, Expo '67, Montreal, Quebec, with Norval Morrisseau

MURALS

1971 Sandy Lake Primary School, Sandy Lake Reserve, Ontario

1973 Sioux Lookout Fellowship and Communication Centre, Sioux Lookout, Ontario (destroyed by fire)

AWARDS

1969 Canada Council Grant

1971 Cultural Development Grant, Department of National Health and
Welfare, Indian Affairs Branch

PUBLICATIONS

Stevens, James and Carl Ray. *Sacred Legends of the Sandy Lake Cree.*
Toronto: McClelland and Stewart, 1971.

COLLECTIONS

Department of Indian Affairs, Ottawa, Ontario

Fort Frances Public Library, Ontario

Manitoba Centennial Corporation, Winnipeg

McMichael Canadian Collection, Kleinburg, Ontario

National Museum of Man, Ottawa, Ontario

New College, University of Toronto, Ontario

Government of Ontario Art Collection, Toronto

Red Lake Friendship Centre, Ontario

Royal Ontario Museum, Toronto

Sioux Lookout Fellowship and Communication Centre, Ontario

Sioux Lookout Public Library, Ontario

Winnipeg Art Gallery, Manitoba

Roy Thomas

Born: 1949 Longlac, Ontario
Art Media: Acrylic on canvas, birch bark, silkscreen prints
Art Education: Self-taught

GROUP EXHIBITIONS

1974	*Contemporary Native Arts of Ontario*, Oakville Centennial Gallery, Ontario
1975	McMichael Gallery, Kleinburg, Ontario
1976	*Contemporary Native Art of Canada – The Woodland Indians*, Royal Ontario Museum, Toronto, for travel to Canada House Art Gallery, London, England, and Aula Luisen Schule, Lahr, West Germany
1976	*Indian Art '76*, Woodland Indian Cultural Educational Centre, Brantford, Ontario
1976	Kar Gallery, Toronto, Ontario
1976	Wells Gallery, Ottawa, Ontario
1978	Nicholas Gallery, Ottawa, Ontario
1978	Hambleton Galleries, Kelowna, B.C.
1978	*Art of the Woodland Indian*, McMichael Canadian Collection, Kleinburg, Ontario
1980	Pollock Gallery, Toronto, Ontario
1980	New College, University of Toronto, Ontario
1982	*Second National Native Art Auction*, Native Canadian Centre, Toronto, Ontario
1983	*Indian Art '83*, Woodland Indian Cultural Educational Centre, Brantford, Ontario
1983	*Last Camp, First Song: Indian Art from the Royal Ontario Museum*, organized by the Thunder Bay National Exhibition Centre, Ontario

SOLO EXHIBITIONS

1966	Nightingale Gallery, Toronto, Ontario
1966	Gallery 103, Toronto, Ontario
1967	Confederation College, Thunder Bay, Ontario
1968	Mary J. Black Library, Fort William, Ontario
1974	Gallery 103, Toronto, Ontario
1974	Kar Gallery, Toronto, Ontario
1978	Wah-sa Gallery, Winnipeg, Manitoba
1978	Pollock Gallery, Toronto, Ontario
1979	Shayne Gallery, Montreal, Quebec
1979	Pollock Gallery, Toronto, Ontario
1980	Shayne Gallery, Toronto, Ontario
1982	Gallery Quan, Toronto, Ontario

COLLECTIONS

Citicorp Canada, Toronto, Ontario
Crown Life Insurance, Toronto, Ontario
Department of Indian Affairs and Northern Development, Ottawa, Ontario
Imperial Oil Collection, Toronto, Ontario
Inuit Gallery, Manheim, Germany
McMichael Canadian Collection, Kleinburg, Ontario
Museum of Man and Nature, Winnipeg, Manitoba
National Museum of Man, Ottawa, Ontario
National Museum of Ethnology, Osaka, Japan
Royal Ontario Museum, Toronto

Saul Williams

Born: 1954 Weagamow Lake Reserve, Ontario
Art Media: Acrylic on canvas
Art Education: Self-taught

SELECTED EXHIBITIONS

1974	*Canadian Indian Art '74*, Royal Ontario Museum, Toronto
1974	*Contemporary Native Arts of Ontario*, Oakville Centennial Gallery, Ontario
1976	*Contemporary Native Art of Canada – The Woodland Indians*, Royal Ontario Museum, Toronto, for travel to Canada House Art Gallery, London, England, and Auila Luisen Schule, Lahr, West Germany
1976	Shayne Gallery, Montreal, Quebec
1977	*Contemporary Native Art of Canada – Triple K Co-operative*, Royal Ontario Museum, Toronto
1977	*Contemporary Indian Art – The Trail from the Past to the Future*, Mackenzie Gallery and Native Studies Programme, Trent University, Peterborough, Ontario
1978	*Art of the Woodland Indian*, McMichael Canadian Collection, Kleinburg, Ontario
1978	Walter Engel Gallery, Toronto, Ontario
1978	*Indian Art '78*, Woodland Indian Cultural Educational Centre, Brantford, Ontario
1979	*Kinder des Nanabush*, from the McMichael Canadian Collection, Kleinburg, Ontario, for Hamburg, West Germany
1979	Nishnawbe Gallery, Toronto, Ontario
1979	Gallery Manfred, Dundas, Ontario
1980	New College, University of Toronto, Ontario
1980	*Indian Art '80*, Woodland Indian Cultural Educational Centre, Brantford, Ontario
1981	*Indian Art '81*, Woodland Indian Cultural Educational Centre, Brantford, Ontario
1982	*Indian Art '82*, Woodland Indian Cultural Educational Centre Brantford, Ontario
1983	*Indian Art '83*, Woodland Indian Cultural Educational Centre, Brantford, Ontario
1983	*Last Camp, First Song: Indian Art from the Royal Ontario Museum*, organized by the Thunder Bay National Exhibition Centre, Ontario

COLLECTIONS

McMichael Canadian Collection, Kleinburg, Ontario
National Museum of Man, Ottawa, Ontario
New College, University of Toronto, Ontario
Royal Ontario Museum, Toronto

PUBLICATIONS

Williams, Saul and Sophia. *Weagamow Notebook*. Toronto: Amethyst Publications, 1978.

Selected Bibliography

Atwood, Margaret. *Survival*. Toronto: House of Anansi Press, 1972.

Black, Mary. "Legends and Accounts of Weagamow Lake." *Rotunda* III, no. 3 (Summer 1970).

Blundell, Valda and Ruth Phillips. "Images of Indianness in Woodland Legend Paintings." Canadian Ethnology Society Conference, May 10, 1982.

Brody, J.J. *Indian Painters, White Patrons*. Albuquerque: University of New Mexico Press, 1971.

"British Columbia Fosters Modern Indian Arts and Crafts." *Saturday Night* LX (September 1945).

Brown, Bill. "Copper Thunderbird: An Ojibway Paints His People's Past." *Weekend Magazine* XLVII, *Toronto Star*, 12 June 1962.

Canadian Guild of Crafts, Quebec. Montreal: Canadian Guild of Crafts, Quebec, 1980.

Cardinal, Harold. *The Unjust Society: The Tragedy of Canada's Indians*. Edmonton: Hurtig Publishers, 1969.

Carpenter, Carole Henderson. "Morrisseau – The Artist as Trickster." *Artmagazine*, November/December 1979.

Carroll, Joy. "The Strange Success and Failure of Norval Morrisseau." *artscanada*, November/December 1964.

Castellano, Marlene. "Vocation or Identity: The Dilemma of Indian Youth." In *The Only Good Indian* by Waubagshig. Toronto: New Press, 1972.

Cinader, Bernhard. *Contemporary Indian Art – The Trail from the Past to the Future*. Peterborough, Ont.: MacKenzie Gallery and Native Studies Programme, 1977.

——. *Contemporary Native Art of Canada – The Woodland Indians*. Toronto: Royal Ontario Museum, 1976.

——. *Contemporary Native Arts of Ontario*. Oakville, Ontario: Oakville Centennial Gallery, 1973.

——. "Manitoulin Island: Explorations of Past, Present, and Future." In *Contemporary Native Art of Canada: Manitoulin Island*. Toronto: Royal Ontario Museum, 1978.

Coleman, Sister Bernard. *Decorative Designs of the Ojibwa of Northern Minnesota*. Washington: Catholic University of America Press, 1947.

Colombo, John Robert, ed. *Windigo: An Anthology of Fact and Fantastic Fiction*. Saskatoon: Western Producer Prairie Books, 1982.

Contemporary Native Art of Canada – Silkscreens from the Triple K Cooperative, Red Lake, Ontario. Toronto: Royal Ontario Museum, 1977.

The Creative Tradition – Indian Handicrafts and Tourist Art. Edmonton: Provincial Museum of Alberta, 1982.

Daniel, Ann. "Norval Morrisseau: Myth and Reality." *The Challenge* (Montreal), 11 December 1966.

Densmore, Frances. *Chippewa Customs*. Smithsonian Institute, Bureau of American Ethnology, Bulletin 86, 1929.

——. "The Native Art of the Chippewa." *American Ethnologist* XLIII, 1941.

——. "Uses of Plants by the Chippewa Indians." *44th Annual Report*, Bureau of American Ethnology, 1928.

Dewdney, Selwyn. "Birth of a Cree-Ojibway Style of Contemporary Art." In *One Century Later*, edited by Ian A.L. Getty and Donald B. Smith. Vancouver: University of British Columbia Press, 1978.

——, ed. *Legends of My People, The Great Ojibway*. Toronto: Ryerson Press, 1965. Written and illustrated by Norval Morrisseau.

——. "Norval Morrisseau." *artscanada*, January/February 1963.

——. *The Sacred Scrolls of the Southern Ojibway*. Toronto: University of Toronto Press for the Glenbow Alberta Institute, 1975.

Dewdney, Selwyn, with Kenneth Kidd. *Indian Rock Paintings of the Great Lakes*. Toronto: University of Toronto Press, 1962; 2nd. ed. 1967.

Dickason, Olive Patricia. *Indian Art in Canada*. Ottawa: Department of Indian Affairs and Northern Development, 1972.

Ehnuiheot. "Ojibway History is Captured in Young Artist's Paintings." I, no. 1 (June 1975).

Evaluation of the Cultural/Educational Centres Program. Prepared by Evalucan Ltd. for Program Evaluation Branch, The Indian and Inuit Affairs Program, The Department of Indian Affairs and Northern Development, 31 December 1978.

Feder, Norman. *Two Hundred Years of North American Indian Art*. New York: Praeger Publishers in Association with the Whitney Museum of American Art, 1971.

Fine Arts Section – Cultural Affairs – Policy Paper. Department of Indian and Northern Affairs, 18 September 1972.

From Our Hands. Toronto: The Art Gallery at Harbourfront, 1982.

Fry, Jacqueline. "Contemporary Arts in Non-Western Societies." *artscanada*, December 1971/January 1972.

——. *Treaties Number 23, 287, 1171: Three Indian Painters of the Prairies*. Winnipeg: Winnipeg Art Gallery, 1972.

Fulford, Robert. "Canadian Indian Art – What Are They Trying to Prove?" *Toronto Star*, 2 June 1973.

Gillies, John. "Communicating Indian Culture through Art." *New Dimensions*, June 1971.

Godderham, Kent, ed. *I Am an Indian*. Toronto: J.M. Dent and Sons, 1969.

Graburn, Nelson H.H., ed. *Ethnic and Tourist Art*. Berkeley: University of California Press, 1976.

Harper, J. Russell. *Painting in Canada: A History*. Toronto: University of Toronto Press, 1966; 2nd. ed. 1977.

Hawley, Carolyn. "The Marketing of Contemporary Indian Art: Northern and Native Issues." Ottawa: Institute of Canadian Studies unpublished paper, 1982.

Haycock, Ronald G. *The Image of the Indian*. Waterloo, Ont.: Waterloo Lutheran University, 1971.

Hickerson, Harold. "Notes on the Post-Contact Origin of the Midewiwin." *Ethno-history* IX, no. 4 (1962).

——. *The Southwestern Chippewa: An Ethnohistorical Study*. American Anthropological Association LIV, no. 3, part 2 (1962).

Highwater, Jamake. *Songs from the Earth: American Indian Painting*. Boston: New York Graphic Society, 1976.

——. *The Sweet Grass Lives On*. New York: Lippincott and Crowell, 1980.

Hilger, Sister Mary Inez. *Chippewa Child Life and Its Cultural Background*. Bureau of American Ethnology, Bulletin 146, 1951.

Hill, Tom. "Canadian Indian Art – Its Death and Rebirth." *Artmagazine*, Summer 1974.

——. "Indian Art is Art, Not an Anthropological Curiosity." 45th Annual Couchiching Conference, on *The Arts in Canada, Today and Tomorrow*. Toronto: Canadian Institute on Public Affairs, 1976.

——. "The Paradox of Norval Morrisseau – A Film Review." *Tawow* IV, no. 4 (Winter 1974).

——. "Politics and Indian Art." *Magazine*, Ontario Association of Art Galleries, Summer/Fall 1979.

Hoffman, W.J. "The Midewiwin or Grand Medicine Society of the Ojibwa." *Bureau of American Ethnology Annual Report* VII, 1886.

Hon. Secretary's Report – Canadian Handicraft Guild, 26 January 1906.

Houle, Robert. "A Firm Statement on the Demoralization of Indian People." *Native Perspective* III, no. 2 (1978).

Hume, Christopher. "The New Age of Indian Art." *Maclean's*, 22 January 1979.

The Indian Arts and Crafts Business: By Your Works Shall Ye Be Known. Report prepared for the Indian Eskimo Economic Development Branch by J. Dockstader, The Laurentian Institute for Social and Economic Development Inc., Ottawa, 1970.

Johnson, Sandra. "Art and Artists." *Winnipeg Free Press*, 30 October 1971.

Johnston, Basil. *Ojibway Heritage*. Toronto: McClelland and Stewart, 1982.

Kubler, George. *The Shape of Time*. New Haven, Conn.: Yale University Press, 1962.

Lang, Andrea. "Curse of the Shamans." *Indian Record*, September/October 1979.

——. "Indian in Transition." *Indian Record*, Winter 1980.

La Violette, F.E. *The Struggle for Survival: Indian Cultures and the Protestant Ethic in B.C.* Toronto: University of Toronto Press, 1973.

Leach, Edmund. *Lévi-Strauss*. London: William Collins and Co., 1970.

Lévi-Strauss, Claude. *The Savage Mind*. London: Weidenfeld Ltd., 1966.

Lyford, Carrie A. *The Crafts of the Ojibwa*. U.S. Office of Indian Affairs, Indian Handicrafts Series No. 5, 1942.

Manuel, George and Michael Posluns. *The Fourth World – An Indian Reality*. Toronto: Collier-Macmillan, 1974.

McLuhan, Elizabeth. *Last Camp, First Song: Indian Art from the Royal Ontario Museum*. Thunder Bay: Thunder Bay National Exhibition Centre and Centre for Indian Art, 1983.

——. "The Myth of the Artist." Unpublished paper, 1979.

——. *Norval Morrisseau: Recent Work*. Thunder Bay: Thunder Bay National Exhibition Centre and Centre for Indian Art, 1983.

——. *Renewal: Masterworks of Contemporary Indian Art from the National Museum of Man*. Thunder Bay: Thunder Bay National Exhibition Centre and Centre for Indian Art, 1982.

——. "The Secularization of Ojibwa Imagery and the Emergence of the Image Makers." In *Contemporary Native Arts of Canada – Manitoulin Island*. Toronto: Royal Ontario Museum, 1978.

Odjig, Daphne, *Tales of Nanabush* (10 vols.). Toronto: Ginn and Co., 1971.

Patterson, Nancy-Lou. *Canadian Native Art*. Toronto: Collier-Macmillan, 1973.

——. "Shaking Tents and Medicine Snakes: Traditional Elements in Contemporary Woodland Art." *Artmagazine*, Summer 1976.

Patterson, Nancy-Lou and Erla Socha. "Recent Trends in Canadian Native Print Making." *Artmagazine*, March/April 1977.

Pelletier, W. and Ted Poole. *For Every North American Indian Who Disappears I Also Begin to Disappear*. Toronto: Neewin Publishing, 1971.

Pohorecky, Zenon S. "Rupestral Art in the Precambrian Shield of Canada." Verhandlungen des XXXVIII, Internationalen Americanistenkongresses, Stuttgart, August 1962.

Pollock, Jack. "Norval Morrisseau – A View from His Agent." *Tawow* IV, no. 4 (Winter 1974).

Pollock, Jack and Lister Sinclair. *The Art of Norval Morrisseau*. Toronto: Methuen Publications, 1979.

A Preliminary Survey of Federal Socio-Economic Research Relating to Human Rights, Minority and Ethnic Groups in Canada. Hawley L. Black, report prepared for Canada Department of Labour, November 1971.

Promotion Requirements of Small Business Services Division and Resources and Industrial Division. For the Indian-Eskimo Economic Development Branch, J.W. Evans, R.H. Belanger, n.d.

A Proposal for a Study of Indian Arts and Crafts in Canada. Submitted to the Indian Affairs Branch by Canadian Consociates Ltd., Toronto, Ontario, 1966.

Quimby, George. *Indian Life in the Upper Great Lakes, 11,000 BC to AD 1800*. Chicago: University of Chicago Press, 1960.

Ravenhill, Alice. *Memoirs of an Educational Pioneer*. Toronto: J.M. Dent and Sons, 1951.

Reimer, Isabel. "Daphne Odjig, Painter." *Chatelaine*, July 1975.

A Report on the Findings of Consultation on Indian Control of the Cultural Education Centres Program. Presented by the National Committee of Indian Cultural Educational Centres, March 1982.

Report by Harry Malcolmson Re: Oil Paintings by Alex Janvier. For the Cultural Affairs Division, The Department of Indian Affairs and Northern Development, n.d.

A Review and Analysis of the Cultural Development Division. K.D. Uppal, Education Branch, Indian and Eskimo Program, 1973.

Ritzenthaler, Robert E. and Pat. *The Woodland Indians of the Western Great Lakes*. New York: American Museum of Natural History Press, 1970.

Rogers, E.S. *The Round Lake Ojibwa*. Occasional Papers of the Art and Archaeology Division of the Royal Ontario Museum, Toronto, No. 5, 1962.

Sacred Circles: Two Thousand Years of North American Indian Art. London: Arts Council of Great Britain, Hayward Gallery, 1976.

Salata, E. "Saul D. Williams – The Woodland Indians' Artist." *Indian Record*, Fall 1980.

"Sandy Lake Artist Gains Recognition." *Dryden Express,* 13 February 1969.

Schwarz, Herbert T. "The Art of Norval Morrisseau." *Vie des Arts*, March 1967.

——. *Tales from the Smokehouse*. Edmonton: Hurtig Publishers, 1974.

——. *Windigo and Other Tales of the Ojibways*. Toronto: McClelland and Stewart, 1969.

Scott, M.O. "Pagan Indians of Canada." *The Canadian Magazine* XV (July 1900).

Sheehan, Carol. *Pipes That Won't Smoke, Coal That Won't Burn: Haida Sculpture in Argillite*. Calgary: Glenbow Museum, 1981.

Southcott, Beth. "Artist from Weagamow Lake." *The Ontario Indian*, June 1982.

——. *The Sacred Drum: The Sacred Art of the Anishnabec*. Unpublished manuscript courtesy of the author.

Sprudzs, Alexandrs. "Cooperative Development Assistance in Support of Arctic Cooperatives." Seminar on Handicraft Development, National Conference Centre, Ottawa, 1975.

Stevens, James. "The Influence of Norval Morrisseau." In *The Work of Norval Morrisseau*. Thunder Bay, Ont.: National Exhibition Centre, 1981.

——. "Interview with Norval Morrisseau." *Artmagazine*, Summer 1974.

——. *Norval Morrisseau: The Ojibway Artist*. Unpublished manuscript, courtesy of the author.

Stevens, James and Carl Ray. *Sacred Legends of the Sandy Lake Cree*. Toronto: McClelland and Stewart, 1971.

A Survey of Contemporary Indians of Canada: Economic, Political, Educational Needs and Policies. H.B. Hawthorn for the Indian Affairs Branch, Ottawa, 1967.

Tawow. "Norval Morrisseau." I, no. 1, Spring 1970.

——. "Odjig." II, no. 1, Spring 1971.

Time Magazine. "Myths and Symbols." 28 September 1962.

——. "Fierce Clarity and Sophistication." 25 August 1975.

Vanderburgh, R.M. "Revitalization Aspects of Manitoulin Island Art." *Abstracts of the Symposium on New Directions in Native American Art History*. 24-26 October 1979, University of New Mexico, Albuquerque.

——: "When Legends Fall Silent Our Ways Are Lost: Some Dimensions of the Study of Aging among Native Canadians." *Abstracts of the Canadian Ethnological Society Conference*, 5-8 March 1981. Ottawa: Canadian Ethnological Society, 1981.

——. *Biographical Notes on Daphne Odjig.* Unpublished manuscript, courtesy of the author.

The White Paper – Statement of the Government of Canada on Indian Policy, 1969. Indian Affairs and Northern Development, Queen's Printer, Cat. No. R32-2469, Ottawa, 1969.

Wright, J.V. *Ontario Prehistory: An Eleven-Thousand-Year Archaeological Outline*. Ottawa: National Museum of Man, 1972.

Photo Credits